Leonie Palmer's
Noosa
Cook
Book

The Blue Group

Acknowledgements

I would like to dedicate this book to my late brother, Rob Palmer, who taught me tenacity, the will to succeed and the need to have laughter in your life.

I would like to thank my fantastic husband, Steven Fisher, for his unconditional support and sorely-tried patience; Jackie Jarratt, who created the impetus to turn an idea into a reality; Phil Jarratt, who pulled out most of his beard in frustration as we worked through this project, and from whom I have learned so much; the whole production team — John, Brett and Michael; and those who contributed recipes and ideas so enthusiastically.

Finally, I also should thank Blake Jewell and Ken Morrison, who brought me here all those years ago, and without whom I may never have found the best recipe of all — Noosa itself.

Leonie Palmer
Noosa Heads, August 1996

A Blue Group Publication

First published in 1996
Reprinted 1996

Noosa Blue Publishing Group Pty Ltd
PO Box 321
Noosa Heads Q 4567
Australia

Design and production:
John Witzig and Brett Geoghegan
Photography: Michael Simmons
Fabric art: Lynne Tanner
Editors: Phil and Jackie Jarratt

National Library of Australia
Cataloguing-in-publication

Palmer, Leonie, 1948-
    Leonie Palmer s Noosa cook book.
    Includes index.
    ISBN 0 646 28258 1.

    1. Cookery, Australian. 2. Noosa Heads (Qld.)
    - Description and travel. I. Title. II. Title:
    Noosa cook book.

641.599432.

Australian distribution by Tower Books
Telephone (02) 9975 5566

Printed in Hong Kong by South China Printing Company (1988) Ltd

INGREDIENTS

INTRODUCTION

I HAVE LONG ENJOYED a complex love affair with this extraordinary part of the world. When I'm in Noosa, there are times when I crave to be somewhere else, and when I'm somewhere else I desperately long to be in Noosa...the smell, the taste, the beauty, the simplicity and the people lure me back. And when I do come back, it is with a sense of frantic anticipation, and Noosa never lets me down.

I get a little bit frustrated with people who scoff at the notion that there is such thing as a Noosa regional cooking style, because nearly a quarter of a century spent working in and around the food industry of this place

tells me otherwise. Ours is a casual cooking style of wit, passion and lazy pleasure; a colourful cuisine touched by the sun, with dishes that are a delight to the eye, a balm for the soul and a sensation to the palate. Our food is an invitation to sunshine.

For what is a regional cooking style if not one that grows from humble beginnings, influenced by climate and inhabitants (both transient and permanent) to become truly representative of a culture? It's not about the smartest, fanciest dishes, served in the finest dining rooms by the snappiest waiters. It's about a place, its people and the way they live their lives. And in Noosa our lives are governed by the pleasure principle.

My Noosa life commenced in the early 1970s. Like so many others, I came here for a holiday, an escape from southern climes to a subtropical paradise, a picturesque coastal village populated mostly by an expatriate community of happy southern escapees. There was also a sprinkling of true blue Queenslanders, who scratched their heads and wished the plague (or at least a bad case of sunburn) on us, so that we would quietly and quickly fade away. Sorry guys, it was too good to leave.

Unlike so many others who came to Noosa, I wasn't a Melbourne girl. I was born in the mining town of Broken Hill, the youngest of three children, and my early years were spent between Melbourne and Adelaide. Finally the family settled in Melbourne and both my senior schooling and nursing degree were completed there.

I wish I could say that, like so many Europeans, my cooking was honed around the hearth in the cosy family kitchen, but it's not the truth. My love of cooking was certainly inherited from my mother, but ours was not that sort of family. I do remember, however, the chestnuts scorching in the open fire that would pop out and frequently burn the carpet, and the shrieks of horror one Sunday morning when the entire family arrived to find me (aged about six) in the kitchen with a brown, oozing sludge spread over every surface. I proudly called it chocolate cake. It was the first thing I ever cooked and the family ate it and declared it okay.

On a trip to London I did the Cordon Bleu cooking course on a whim. It cemented for me the idea that cooking was a passion, that there was so much to learn.

Back in Melbourne I fell in love and neither the career I already had, nor the ones that beckoned could keep me from following him to Noosa. It was a Bogart-inspired Caribbean fantasy, or something like that. Adventure called.

It is no exaggeration to say that most of the streets were unpaved. What is now the ritzy residential enclave of Noosa Sound was mangrove swamp, and the original river mouth did its tidal, seasonal thing at the end

Above: Up the lazy river. A classic Noosa riverboat ferries tourists in the 1930s.

Opposite page: Bathers on Main Beach, 1920s.

of the caravan park that is now the Noosa Woods reserve (our most spectacular picnic area). There were no signs along the Bruce Highway directing attention to this luxury hotel or that new waterfront development because these things did not yet exist.

I particularly remember the old river mouth and the Woods caravan park because my first restaurant in Noosa was Dooley's, right at the bottom of Hastings Street. When the summer rains and the Christmas king tides collided in happy conjunction, the park would flood. On many occasions, as we cleared up the mess after the evening's splatter of batter circus that produced mountains of doily-lined cane baskets of crisply fried prawns and plum chilli sauce, we'd open up the concertina doors and let in the drenched campers for a soothing rum and Coke and a dry booth to sleep in.

Noosa was like that in those days. Yes, even then we ate and drank, and did so very well. With gusto, even. There'd been restaurants and guest house dining rooms since Laguna House opened its doors in 1906, but in the '70s the eating establishments were steered by a crazy

The essential elements of Noosa cooking: fresh produce presented with style and simplicity. Whole fish by Leonie.

Above: Noosa from the air, 1950s.

Opposite: The author as a sweet, young innocent.

bunch of people from all over the globe who had nothing in common but the discovery of paradise where the Noosa River meets the sea.

Our social interaction consisted mainly of dining in each other's restaurants on the abundant, cheap and fresh local seafood. A typical night's feast would be black bean and chilli crab with freshly-baked bread and plenty of wine. At Barry's Bistro, pioneer chef Barry Ritter would serve us his version of these dishes and we'd sit and eat in the most fabulous beach setting on the Australian east coast.

When it came to running a restaurant, Barry was the old pro in a sea of rank amateurs like myself. Of course, he'd had a head start, arriving with his parents in the early 1960s to run a beachfront motel. But to this day I can picture his look of wry amusement as we rolled into town, opened our cute little "hole in the wall" restaurants and ran them with a basic philosophy of she'll be right.

Food and wine travelled across the street (and even across town) as we struggled with the idea of being serious by night and frivolous by day. In our minds we were all on a holiday, life seemed so much simpler. You could drive off and leave your banking bag on top of your car and get it back intact. (True story.) We had no idea of the ebb and flow of the tourist trade, and therefore ordered too much or not enough. Fortunately, such was the camaraderie of those days that everyone was prepared to share. And as our reputations grew, so did our understanding of how things worked. One thing that hasn't changed is inflation – in this case the number of people we claimed to have fed each night. Over late night raves in our favourite drinking holes, we would exchange outrageous customer stories and often add at least one nought to the number we had served.

At Coco's, up at the gates to the Noosa National Park, Swiss-born Pierre Otth had just arrived, and was destined never to unpack his formal European attire. He fed us sensationally on fish bonne femme in a claypot and other dishes that were probably as new to him as they were to us. The koalas, happy for the company, would hang out of the trees, checking it all out.

Meanwhile, French-born Luc Turschwell was busy at Belmondo's, spicing up delights we had never seen before, with a touch of Moroccan and a dash of French style, along with pistachio nuts by the barrel, served atop warm flat bread.

Richard and Fay Jones served up great Mexican food from a doll's house in Hastings Street which they called Harvest, and Suzie Miekle at Forty Baskets served (you got it) seafood baskets with a beach view.

There were others, many others, who touched us with their talent and style and moved on. Their presence is felt in this book, but it is really a tribute to those chefs, cooks, entrepreneurs, madmen and adventurers who came and stayed, and helped to create a food style to match a lifestyle – one which is recognised all over Australia today as being quintessentially Noosa.

Leonie K Rae

THE PLACE

WHEN I ARRIVED in Noosa in 1973, there was a commonly held perception that food had just been invented, and that the locals would line our pockets with money and bow down and thank us for introducing them to this sybaritic delight. Not that we thought we were restaurateurs – it was just a way of getting next week's rent.

But, in fact, Noosa had been dining out for generations, and if not well, then at least substantially. The tradition of home-cooked meals (often local seafood) served unpretentiously in austere dining rooms, began with the Tewantin Hotel and the Royal Mail, also in Tewantin.

Because Noosa was in those days basically an island, the staging point for visitors was Tewantin, a timber town some six kilometres up the Noosa River. From the turn of the century, overnight visitors were treated to "fish suppers", singalongs and traditional bush hospitality.

By 1905 there were five houses at Noosa Heads, two of which were guest houses. These were Hay's Bayview (now Halse Lodge) and Bainbridge's Laguna House. In 1906 Laguna House was bought by

The most beautiful sunsets in the world. Looking west down Hastings Street.

Above: The ferry from Tewantin lands early tourists at the rivermouth for the courtesy bus to Hastings Street lodgings.

Left: Tait's Royal Mail Hotel, Tewantin, in 1919, when it was a staging house on the Cobb & Co route to Gympie.

Opposite page: Laguna House on Hastings Street, 1920s.

John Donovan, a foodie of his day, who saw the market potential and served classic seafood combos from river and ocean, teamed with fresh bread baked on the premises and lashings of salty butter. Patrons could hear the ocean waves crashing onto the shore behind the sand-hills, as they tucked into their sand flathead or river whiting.

While Laguna House remained the number one dining room in town (and also the party hub), during the war years the Massoud clan – local fishermen since the early years of the century – went into the restaurant game with Maussoud's Favourite Cafe. This modest establishment (the building, somewhat revamped, still stands today as a Mexican BYO) stood like a beacon on the Noosa river-front. Mt Ninderry, a few miles to the south near Yandina, was an important jungle training station for the AIF, and a regular exercise for the soldiers was to travel cross-country to the Noosa River, where they would be picked up by barge. Fortuitously, many of them made their exit from the wilderness somewhat adjacent

Top: Dusk at the river mouth.

Left: Maisy Monsour with three generations of the Massoud clan, Noosaville, 1996.

A Noosa River mud crab,
straight out of the pot and ready to be tied.

to Massoud's Favourite Cafe, where they knew that a groaning plate of fresh fish or Cooroy steak, a rollicking good time around the pianola, and maybe even a cold beer, would be waiting.

The Favourite Cafe's first chef, Maisy Monsour, told Noosa Blue Magazine in 1991: "It was the happiest, busiest time of my life. All that work never did me any harm at all. I fried the fish in olive oil. The steaks were grilled on a hot plate, wiped over with an oil rag first."

The first Massouds to come to Noosa were Jiddy and Edith, Lebanese immigrants from a fishing tradition. With their sons, George, Ivan, Bill and Phillip, they established Noosa's first commercial fishing operation, and also took early tourists on beach fishing expeditions on the North Shore. Their influence on Noosa seafood has been evident for more than half a century, perhaps no more evident than in the early

1990s when Brett Massoud ran Bratpacker's Cafe in Noosaville and presented the freshest and some of the most original fish dishes in town.

If the Massoud's Favourite Cafe was the hub of culinary good times throughout the 1940s, then in the 1960s and '70s that honour went to Barry's On The Beach. The only real restaurant on the beachfront, Barry's boasted picture windows that looked out on the vast expanse of beach by day and by night the moonlight twinkling on the bay and the odd car light coming down the National Park road.

Top: The wide expanse of Main Beach, Noosa, 1937.

Above: North Shore catch, 1930s.

BARRY'S FAMOUS COCONUT PRAWNS (C.1970)

Serves 6

24 fresh green prawns
flour
Carnation milk
shredded coconut
little tiny hats
umbrellas

Take the freshest peeled and veined king prawns with tails on, 4 per person. Dust in flour and dip in Carnation milk, because it doesn't sour. Wrap in shredded coconut.

Heat oil in deep open pan, $^2/_3$ full, to 180°C/350°F. Fry until just cooked and golden tanned. Remember to drain the prawns on kitchen paper.

Serve on a scallop shell with lemon wedges and (of course) chilli plum sauce. If you want to be picky, use 2 beaten eggs in place of the Carnation milk.

The end of an era.

Inside, mine host Barry Ritter and right hand man "Mumbles" Walker bustled around the kitchen, the tables groaned with good food, good wine, starched white cloths and polished glasses. The bar buzzed with raucous good humour and relationships made in heaven were cemented (and sometimes ruined), and rumour turned to fact before your very eyes on those late nights of legend.

Barry seemed to have everything. His cellar was well-organised and impressive in quality, his cool room was chockers with well-hung beef, and better stocked than most of us had ever dreamed of – indeed, it was bigger than most of our kitchens, and better constructed.

Barry's Steak la Mer, put on the menu as a bit of a parody of the "surf and turf" dish to be found in

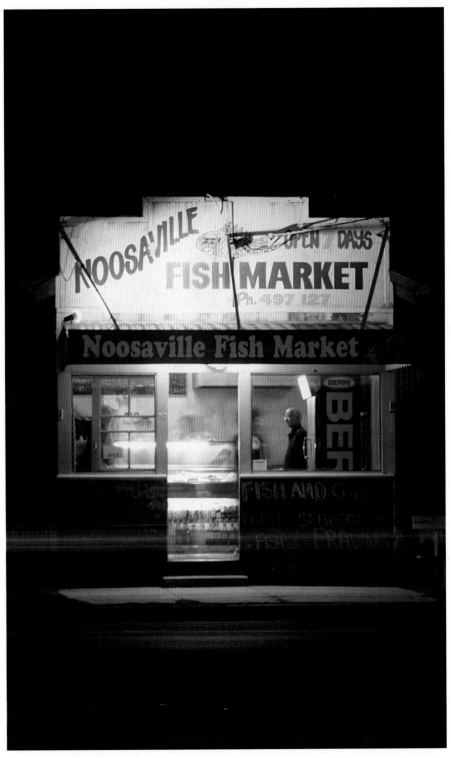

Same as it ever was, Noosa's funkiest fish shop.

LEONIE'S FISH 'N CHIPS

Serves 4-6

8-12 fresh white fish fillets bones removed,
about 80gm/3oz each
2 lemons, cut into wedges
peanut or grapeseed oil for deep frying

Batter

plain flour
level teasp of sweet paprika powder
$1/2$ teasp ground white pepper
water

Sift plain flour, paprika and pepper into a good sized bowl and whisk in enough water to make a batter that pours off your finger leaving a thin film. Stand, covered with cling wrap, for at least half an hour.

Lightly flour the fish, brushing off any excess, dip fish completely in batter, shaking off excess and cook in oil until golden brown – hold by end until sealed and then it won't stick to the pan. Drain on kitchen paper.

Fill a deep-sided, wide-topped pan with oil to $2/3$ full and bring to 190°C/375°F.

Chips

6 potatoes (Kennebee)

Peel and cut into 1 $1/2$ cm batons and soak in cold water for 10 minutes. Pat dry with kitchen cloth to remove starch. Blanch in hot oil until lightly cooked (pale). Drain on kitchen paper. Allow to cool.

Cook the drained cooled chips again until golden brown and crisp. Drain and keep warm while you deep fry the fish.

LEONIE'S BLACK BEAN AND CHILLI CRAB

Serves 2-4 (or 1 in my case!)

2 large fresh sand crabs, or 1 large mudcrab
1 tablesp canned salted black beans
2 large cloves of garlic (1 crushed and 1 chopped finely)
1 tablesp light soy sauce   1 teasp sugar
4 tablesp peanut oil   4 slices fresh ginger
$^2/_3$ cup hot water
2 teasp cornflour mixed in 1 tablesp cold water
4 spring onions, chopped in long pieces
1 teasp sambal oelek (or fresh chillies to taste)

Have your fishmonger clean your crabs or wash well, remove hard shell and fibrous tissue. ˒

Chop and break crab into 4 pieces, separate larger claws from the body and crack shells of claws.

Rinse black beans in a strainer under cold water for 1 minute, drain. Mash beans well and mix with crushed garlic, soy sauce, sugar and sambal oelek.

Heat oil in large frying pan or wok and fry chopped garlic and ginger until they start to brown, then remove from pan.

Over high heat fry the pieces of crab, turning constantly until shells are bright red, about 5 minutes. Remove crabs from pan.

Add black bean mixture to the oil and fry 1 minute, then add hot water, crab pieces and stir well. Cover pan and cook about 3 minutes. Stir in cornflour mix, stir until boiling and slightly thickened. Toss in spring onions.

Serve at once in a big bowl with a separate large bowl of jasmine rice for the table, a plate for the shells and lots of paper napkins and finger bowls with lemon.

clubland, turned out to be his second most successful dish (after his famous coconut prawns), with the restaurant doing 40 a night out of 50 main courses.

Barry could tell you the cost of a bum on a seat, right down to the air-conditioning component. The rest of us had trouble working out that air-conditioning could actually increase our business! That was why we were there every night for a late drink – it was so wonderfully cool.

Apart from its obvious seafood bounty, Noosa had much to recommend it to potential restaurateurs. Hastings Street ran parallel to a beautiful north-facing beach, and at one end there was a national park and at the other the river-mouth surrounded by bush. Noosa had the most pleasing aspect of any coastal town in Australia. Behind the beach-front tourist

LEONIE'S GRILLED WHOLE KING SNAPPER

Clean, scale and rinse.

Make a few incisions diagonally with the point of a knife so that it cooks evenly and the skin does not burst - if the fish is large keep the fire lower (or fish further away from the fire 150-200mm (6-8inch), cooking time varies.

Marinate in olive oil, lemon juice, salt and pepper.

To this you can add a little crushed garlic, fresh tomato pulp, chopped herbs, fennel, basil, oregano or sage, 2-3 anchovies or white wine vinegar. Flour the fish. Heat grill until very hot and place fish on hot plate.

Give the first side longer than the second, turn once or twice if fish firm enough. (Hinged double grill makes this easier).

LEONIE'S FISH SOUP

Serves 8

2kg/4$\frac{1}{2}$lb fresh white fish fillets or steaks, cut into big pieces
2 onions chopped
125ml/4$\frac{1}{2}$fl oz olive oil
3 cloves garlic finely chopped
1kg/2$\frac{1}{4}$lb tomatoes (Roma when available) peeled
and chopped (or tinned)
1 teasp sugar
sea salt and pepper
$\frac{1}{2}$ teasp saffron threads
1 bunch chopped flat leaf parsley
water
slices of thick grilled bread.

In a wide casserole or large shallow pan fry the onions in oil until soft, then add the garlic and fry until the aroma rises.

Add the tomatoes, sugar and saffron threads

Season and add 1litre/36fl oz water

Simmer 15 minutes

Put in all the fish, make sure enough liquid to half cover the fish, if necessary add more water. Gently simmer for about 20 minutes until fish is done, adjust seasoning to taste. Add the parsley and serve with grilled or toasted bread.

If you are adding other seafoods, mussels etc, put them in before the fish.

strip lay a lush and fertile hinterland ideal for growing produce, but at that time much of the land was under cane and the only items of local produce that seemed to find their way to the table were those subtropical perennials, bananas, paw paws and pineapples.

We did most of our food shopping at one of the two greengrocers in Noosa Junction, then a straggly shopping disaster over the hill and far away, where we'd fight over the few lettuce and pock-marked tomatoes. Lemons, so essential for our seafood dishes, seemed to cost almost as much as the fish, and were never in such plentiful supply that you could pile them up in lush displays in the restaurant. Milk, cream and eggs came from the corner store or the town's only supermarket. Tewantin had a poultry farm where you could buy eggs (although I don't remember buying chooks there) but it seemed like such a long way to go in those days. The ubiquitous canned goods formed a fairly large part of our kitchen shelves and were the basis of many a sauce which in those days was deemed perfectly acceptable.

We did our bulk buying of canned goods and flour, sugar and coffee in the old sugar cane town of Nambour on the Bruce Highway. The occasional Brisbane trip – then a full day expedition – would complete the picture, and I remember many a long evening drive home with a

Commercial fishermen still work the Noosa River and the outside reefs.

Leonie's Mussels In A Quick Broth

Serves 4-6

You need a quick broth for mussels, because when they come along – fresh, small, black mussels that is – you want to devour them instantly.

2kg/4$\frac{1}{2}$lb black mussels
1 medium brown onion, peeled and diced
3 cloves garlic, finely chopped
freshly ground black pepper to taste
$\frac{1}{2}$ cup of dry white wine
1$\frac{1}{2}$ cups of good tomato sauce or 1$\frac{1}{2}$ cups tomato juice
$\frac{1}{2}$ bunch each of Italian parsley, coriander and chives,
all finely chopped
virgin olive oil

Scrub and remove beard from mussels and place in a bowl of cold water for 10 minutes or longer. This will contribute greatly to the juices you'll want to mop up.

Pour a little virgin olive oil into a large cooking pot that has a tight fitting lid. Briefly fry the onion and garlic until soft. Add the white wine, tomato juice or sauce and ground black pepper.

Put in the mussels, cover with the lid and let steam on high heat for about 5 minutes. Give the pot a good shake, another 5 minutes, another shake and your mussels should be opened and ready to serve.

Lift off lid, take off half shell, put into one big bowl. Pour over the juice and throw in the chopped herbs. Share out the mussels, you'll need a ladle for the juice and plenty of bread to soak it up. (They say don't eat the unopened ones.)

Fried Prawn Cakes

250gm/9oz fresh raw prawns, shelled and minced
1 clove of garlic finely chopped
2 spring onions finely chopped
$\frac{1}{2}$ teasp salt
60gm/2$\frac{1}{4}$oz plain flour
4 teasp Manzarillo or Fino sherry
olive oil to deep fry

Mix together garlic, prawns, onion, salt, flour, sherry and add enough water (about 150ml/5fl oz) to make a thick pouring batter. Cover with cling wrap and stand for 1 hour.

Heat about 5cm/2inch of oil over high heat and drop in teaspoonsful of the prawn batter. Watch out, the moisture can make the batter spit.

Cook 1 minute each side until brown and crisp. Drain on kitchen paper and serve, preferably with a Spanish garlic mayonnaise.

load of food on the back-seat and a kilo of fresh pistachios on my lap, most of which would be devoured on the three-hour journey. Too often I remember seeing the lights of Noosaville come into focus with dry mouth, salty lips and a car littered with shells.

I also used to spend time scouting around the hills and valleys for local suppliers of fresh fruit and vegetables, and on these journeys often ran into true locals who had never been down to "The Heads". They knew Noosa as the "seventh sandbar", an obstacle to river traffic rather than a real town. Hastings Street was a settlement which would obviously be washed away with the first decent cyclone.

One of the characters we bought from regularly was Steve, the crazy strawberry man on the Cooroy road. His strawberries were first class, but it was always a battle to get out of there without a bottle or two of his strawberry wine.

Our seafood supplies came from the local fish board at Tewantin, looking straight down the river, with a cute little fish and chip shop (still operating today) right at the front gate. Those were the days when I'd buy a bin of calamari and the boys would throw in the Moreton Bay bugs for free – they hadn't yet attained star status. There was also quite a bit of black market dealing (known to us as "blackfish") with characters who talked out of the sides of their mouths, did the deal off the back of the ute and disappeared with the cash. But the deals were usually good and the produce still quivering. Occasionally we'd make the trip to the deep water port of Mooloolaba, where the catch was more regular and there was a greater variety of species. The fish were sold at auction, guaranteeing higher prices, so our journeys there were infrequent.

As time went by and more restaurants became established in Noosa, our suppliers began to realise that they would have to tailor their supply to our demands. The farmers and market gardeners of the region began to see that there were other things they could grow and sell to us at the kitchen door. Cos lettuce, rosemary, Italian parsley, lemon grass, chives, coriander, chillies...all these products eventually became available locally and part of our regional cuisine.

The land began to yield a bounty as diverse as any available anywhere in the world, and our Noosa food began to take on a style of its own.

THE INFLUENCES

I T SEEMS TO ME that any place in the world is really the sum total of the experiences of its locals and the influence of the foreigners who pass through. This is particularly so in Noosa.

For me, travels to the Mediterranean (particularly Italy and Spain) and to Jamaica taught me a lot about food with passion. I began to realise that lifestyle and climate were an integral part of what you ate. So, as I grew in confidence as a restaurateur in Noosa, I began to apply some of those lessons. But what really brought me out of my inherent Australian-British food fixation was the arrival in town of two larger than life characters.

Above: Style pioneer Luc Turschwell, still Gallic after all these years.

Right: Pierre Otth, doing what he does best.

Luc Turschwell, a Frenchman brought up in North Africa, and Pierre Otth, a Swiss-Frenchman, brought with them a life-time of personal and professional culinary influences from their native lands and their many travels.

When Luc Turschwell was a little boy growing up in North Africa, he would help his mother bake bread in a cast iron camp oven. When he came home from school he would eat two slabs of bread brushed in garlic and olive oil with a chilli in between. Coming of age in the 1960s, Luc did what so many of our

generation did – packed a rucksack and hit the denim trail across
Europe and Asia, eventually arriving in Darwin on a tramp steamer from
Timor and working his way overland to Sydney. After several years in
the rag trade, he and his Australian wife Lyn and their young sons set
off on a round-Australia trip, and got as far as Noosa. Ho hum, same old
story, fell in love with the place and stayed.

I met Luc soon after my own arrival in town, on his first job, which was
to mind a cafe called Chanson de Mer while the owner went to Europe.
He was a dashing, extroverted, bridge and chess playing character of the
type you seldom came across in an Australian country town – which was
what Noosa still was.

By 1975 Luc and I faced each other across Hastings Street. I had
Dooley's on the beach side of the street (which I originally managed for
an Irish rogue named John Michael Patrick O'Flaherty, and eventually
acquired in lieu of wages) and he was across the way at Belmondo's. We
served traditional fish and chips twice a day while Luc's Mediterranean-
style cafe was open continuously on the sunny side of the street. Around
dusk every day the smell of Luc's Moroccan spices would waft across
the street, luring a clientele hungry for a change of flavours.

On my nights off I would often be drawn to Belmondo's. It was a
quaint little cottage with the internal walls knocked out, a roughly-
paved courtyard with blue umbrellas and a dimly lit inner sanctum

---

LUC'S SIMPLY EYE FILLET

Take a piece of cleaned eye fillet and slice 2.5cm/1inch thick,
3 slices per person.

On a hot grill, quickly criss-cross and grill, keeping it fairly rare.
Rest the meat for 5-10 minutes.

Slice a red ripe tomato in 3 slices, place on plate, top with the
grilled eye fillet, one per slice, sprinkle with crushed black
pepper, basil and a dash of olive oil.

where patrons sat on cushions, drank pastis and played backgammon until the wee hours.

At Belmondo's breakfast didn't have to consist of bacon and eggs – how about a delicately-spiced compote of Turkish figs and fresh yoghurt, or perhaps a choukchouka, a wonderfully stewed tomato dish that I salivate over even as I write today. Luc's all-day fare included sates, merguez sausages and capsicum-filled warm flat bread, dishes which had never been seen in Noosa before.

LEONIE'S PAN BAGNAT

A dish of Provence that makes me think of Luc and Pierre and their influences.

crusty French baguette
1 clove garlic, cut in half
olive oil
wine vinegar
500gm/18oz sliced ripe tomatoes
1 onion finely sliced
1 green pepper deseeded, sliced and grilled
1 red pepper deseeded, sliced and grilled
2 hard boiled eggs sliced
6 anchovy fillets
6 black olives stoned and sliced
sea salt and pepper to taste
(Can replace the anchovies with small tin tuna or finely sliced fresh ham)

Slice baguette lengthwise - pull out a little soft bread from centre. Rub the inside of each half with garlic, pour on a few drops of vinegar and plenty of olive oil, salt and pepper. Fill the loaf with tomatoes, onions, peppers, egg, anchovies and olives. Season.

Press the top of the loaf on like a lid. Wrap in tin foil and put under a weight or tie with string for 1-2 hours to allow the juices to seep through to the bread. Slice and serve.

LUC'S CHOUKCHOUKA

4 red capsicums, 3 ripe tomatoes, 2 cloves garlic, chilli (optional),
olive oil, salt and pepper.

Clean and seed the capsicum and chop into small chunks. In a
heavy pot put a little olive oil. Put in the capsicum and whole garlic,
just to perfume. Cook until soft, with the chilli and a little water.

Peel tomatoes, seed and chop coarsely. Add to the capsicum and
season to taste. Cover and cook until a jam-like consistency.

If you like you can add a broken egg, and you have a piperade,
the choukchouka with a poached egg on top.

Above: Luc's Moroccan fish dish.

Right: A sunset barbie with friends at the river mouth.

Below: Proud father of Pasquale (and Jean-Pierre, Mischa and Zac).

BUGS BELMONDO

Moreton Bay bugs, lemon juice, butter,
chopped parsley and basil, splash of Pernod,
Dijon mustard and salt and pepper to taste.

Cut the Moreton Bay bugs in ½ lengthwise, clean and sprinkle with lemon juice. Mix together remaining ingredients and spread over the bug meat.

Sit the bugs on the chargrill, shell side down. As the shell burns a little it creates the flavour and the bug poaches gently in the shell.

Take off when the bug meat is just cooked and serve immediately.

This was the grill chef's nightmare, as so many went onto the fire at once. Such was the popularity of the dish.

TARTE TATIN

(Overturned Tart)

Sweet shortcrust pastry, enough to top 30cm/12inch pan

Take 8 big cooking apples, peel and cut in ½ - take out most of the seeds (leave some for flavour).

Combine 340gm/12oz sugar, 170gm/6oz butter and dash of brandy in pan and saute apples rounded side down until caramelised on the outside but not cooked through. The apples should be packed in tightly - pan must have handle that can go in the oven (200°C/400°F).

In this same pan lay the pastry over the apples - packing in around the edges with the fingers - when cooked 15-20 minutes take out and turn upside down. serve with the caramel juices and ice-cream. (You can also use pears for this recipe).

LUC'S MIDNIGHT EXPRESS

Simply take a parfait glass, layer chopped date pieces and fresh bananas and pour cream over the top to fill. Stand for 24 hours in the fridge. To serve sprinkle with cinnamon.

LUC'S ESCABECHE (MOROCCAN FISH)

Use either whole fish, fillets or sardines.
Chilli powder, paprika, garlic and wine vinegar.

Rub salt into the fish, flour and fry in oil in a shallow pan. Remove fish from pan and rest in a warm place.

Remove oil and deglaze the pan with a shot of wine vinegar.

In a bowl mix with the fingers the crushed garlic, paprika, chilli powder, pinch of flour and a dash of water to make a wet paste, pour this into the hot pan and reduce slightly until it has melded and pour over the fish. Season to taste with salt and pepper. Eat hot or cold, especially good made with sardines.

Around the same time Pierre Otth arrived in town. He too had come in through Darwin on the denim trail – obviously a hole in the fence! Classically trained in Europe, Pierre's travels in Asia had added a new dimension to both his cooking and his personality. He visited a hippie commune at North Arm in the Noosa hinterland and soon became caught up in the freewheeling lifestyle, cheap eating and easy climate of Noosa.

He says: "One day I was sitting around at Granite Bay in the nude, of course, playing backgammon, and a fellow came up the beach and asked if I was French. He was nude too, of course, so we had a chat and it transpired he had a friend who had just taken over a restaurant and he wanted some one to fix it up and run it. So I took the job. It had been set up as a Japanese restaurant and the kitchen was very different to anything I was used to, so I improvised a lot and created dishes that combined French influences with Japanese cooking methods. Some of the food was wonderful, but I must say at that time there was a little bit of resistance towards anything too unusual in food, and I had to tone it down a little. This was the first Coco's."

Barbie, Pierre style.

Coco's, at the gates to the National Park, was a simple cottage not unlike Belmondo's, and it also had the same allure of the unknown. Pierre himself was a creature from another planet – a Balinese sarong wrapped around his middle, a shark's tooth hanging from his neck, bare-chested most of the time and often taken for, in his own words, "a dirty foreign hippy".

Coco's quickly became the vortex of the known universe – at least for us. Musician Colin McLachlan slept in his panel van parked outside the restaurant and used its toilet and bathroom. By night he sang for his supper. Crystal (no surnames in those days) worked in the Balinese sarong shop in Hastings Street and would walk around to Coco's every evening for dinner with her boyfriend. After dinner they would walk on to Granite Bay where they lived (comfortably but illegally) in a tent.

Pierre Otth in 1996.

The dope dealers had arrived in town, colourful, free-spending and full of energy which was contagious. As Noosa's one policeman lived in Tewantin, it was easy to keep tabs on him, and if the cat was asleep out came the mouses!

Another of Coco's colourful regulars was Dook (later of Dook's Wine Bar) whose first booking – made by placing your name on the black-board outside – was for five people. Dook was so impressed with his dinner that he boasted to Pierre that he would return with 10 people. He was as good as his word, and after another great night he told Pierre: "Next time 20!" Another great night, another promise. Dook filled the restaurant with 40 people and officially ended the challenge.

FISH BONNE FEMME IN A CLAY POT

Having inherited the pots with the restaurant (Coco's), Pierre invented this recipe which achieved legendary status and can still today cause eyes to glaze and lips to smack.

For each pot, one serve: –
a little chopped onion
one thick fish fillet, very fresh (150gm/5oz)
4 fresh, chopped mushrooms
about 50ml/2fl oz white wine
about 100ml/4fl oz cream
butter to grease the clay pot
salt and pepper to taste

Butter the clay pot and put in a little onion. Lay fish fillet on the top. Coral trout is a good fish variety to use. Add mushrooms, and season lightly.

Add white wine and cream to reach about half way up the fish. (This is the tricky bit, to have the right amount of liquid to be reduced to a sauce consistency when the fish is cooked.)

Put the top on the clay pot, place in a moderate oven and cook until perfect, probably about 20 minutes.

Pierre at Belmondo's, about 1980.

PRAWNS IN THE SHELL FLAMBE

Take fresh uncooked prawns, shell and all. Into a hot pan put some garlic, a little butter, wine and herbs. Add the prawns. Flame the pan with cognac and reduce as the prawns cook. They are cooked when pink all over. A messy wonderful dish with a fantastic sauce, as the heads add the flavour.

PERNOD PRAWNS

Peel and devein uncooked fresh prawns, then toss into a hot pan with a little butter and fine chopped onion. Flame with Pernod, add just a touch of cream, put on a lid and reduce cream just a little.

PEPPERED TUNA

Lightly sear the tuna ($1\frac{1}{2}$cm/$\frac{1}{2}$inch thick) in crushed pepper and lemon thyme, then flambe in cognac and white wine. Pierre likes it blue and the most he will cook it is medium rare, "otherwise you might as well buy it in the can!". (Cook about 2 minutes each side for medium rare.)

Serve with a simple green salad and crusty bread.

Tuna and mascarpone rolls.

The presence in Noosa of these two flamboyant Europeans, Luc and Pierre, soon attracted more like-minded souls, passionate about food as part of a leisure lifestyle. The style of their restaurants soon gathered a strong local following. Music was part of the equation too – both Coco's and Belmondo's featured local musicians in jam sessions – but it was mainly the open-hearted acceptance of new flavours by people who had been brought up on plainer fare.

The new food influences in town certainly had a major impact on me. They reminded me of my own travels and made me realise that anything was possible in this context. I suddenly felt I had the freedom to experiment with food. Also, the Europeans had thrown down the gauntlet and I had to take up the challenge. I didn't mind sharing my customers, but I wasn't going to lose them. And the sharing wasn't restricted to customers. Before long we were also sharing chefs and waiters.

On the menu at Dooley's, my famous peppered prawns began to appear threaded on sate sticks and the creamy peppercorn sauce gave way to peanut, coconut and chilli, a sauce recipe taught to me by Louie Knoll, a chef I poached from Belmondo's. Our curries were no longer dusted with Keen's curry powder, but blessed with fresh and fragrant spice mixtures roasted in our kitchen. The cute little pumpkins I would

Tuna Mascarpone Rolls

200gm/7oz raw tuna
150gm/5oz mascarpone
1 teasp lemon juice
100gm/3$^{1}/_{2}$oz rocket leaves
3 tablesp caper salsa
2 tablesp capers
extra virgin olive oil
balsamic vinegar

Slice the tuna into thin slices.

Mix the mascarpone with lemon juice and caper salsa. Place mixture in piping bag with nozzle large enough for salsa to fit through. Pipe mixture in a line on each slice of tuna, roll up sausage style.

Refrigerate until ready to serve.

Toss rocket leaves lightly through a little oil and balsamic vinegar, lay the rolls into the rocket and scatter with capers.

Caper salsa

1 celery heart diced finely
1 red capsicum, roasted, skinned and diced
2 tomatoes, seeded and diced
$^{1}/_{2}$ spanish onion, diced
2 tablesp capers, chopped
4 tablesp extra virgin olive oil

Mix all ingredients together in a bowl. Marinate at least two hours. Seal in jar and keep in refrigerator.

RICOTTA CHEESE DESSERT

Serves 6

500gm/18oz fresh Ricotta
4 eggs, separated
3 tablesp plain flour
250gm/9oz sugar
1teasp ground cinnamon
$\frac{1}{2}$ teasp ground nutmeg
grated rind of 3 limes
5 tablesp brandy
icing sugar

Mash ricotta and beat well with egg yolks. Stir in sifted flour, sugar, nutmeg and cinnamon, lime zest, brandy and mix well. Stiffly beat the egg whites and fold into mixture and pour into an oiled and floured 25cm/10inch cake tin.

Bake 180°C/350°F for about 40 minutes middle of oven until just firm.

Serve hot or cold dusted with icing sugar and the strawberries with lime and sugar.

STRAWBERRIES WITH LIME & SUGAR

Serves 6

1kg/2$\frac{1}{4}$lb approx of fresh strawberries (I like small ones best). Mascerate for 20 minutes in juice of 3 limes and 6 tablesp raw sugar.

Serve with Ricotta Cheese Desert.

---

hollow out and put the curry in, became the curry itself, studded with roasted cashews and shredded coconut.

All this heady activity rang many changes in Noosa, as did the developer's hammer. Buildings were being knocked down and new ones would appear in their place, sometimes before you even noticed. The look of Hastings Street, and the whole area, began to change. We began to seek new challenges, new businesses, and some of us opened our second, more professional, more up-to-the-minute premises. Some sold their originals and started again.

With a couple of partners, I opened The Gallery Wine Bar, soon to be renamed Rio's, a Peter Allen-inspired upstairs, clubby, champagne-swilling, cocktail-shaking nightspot where we served as much food at the bar as at the tables. Real estate agents rubbed shoulders with solicitors, rogues and cads, bounders sought solace with models and musos, developers outdid drug dealers (so I'm told), and waitresses would appear on roller skates, in clown suits or doing Bette Midler routines, all the while making sure the grilled lamb cutlets, roasted baby chickens and Moreton Bay bugs made it to the tables on time.

Luc had moved on to Gaston's, an amazingly-romantic cane-encrusted and stylish cafe at Sunshine Beach. Pierre was at The Wharf, a sensational white and handcrafted timber bar and restaurant which sat right on the Noosa River, looking down towards the mouth and across to the untamed North Shore. And so this rag-tag band of freewheelers moved into the next era. We were now more professional, more organised, more acclaimed and still passionate. Our produce was better, our wines more palatable, our acts more refined.

Like most Australian country towns, Noosa had its own Chinese restaurant, and we had all picked up on black beans, soy sauce and ginger. Proprietor John Mew (China World, later Chinois) may have been Noosa's pioneer in the proliferation of Asian cooking taking place throughout Australia in the 1980s, when coriander, lemon grass and kaffir lime leaves became familiar names, and fish sauce came to mean more than meuniere.

THE RESTAURANTS

WHEN I STARTED to throw around ideas for this section of the book, I was surprised at how many restaurants that I would term "landmark" or "legendary" this small part of the world has given us. Of course, many of them are no longer with us, but they live on in the memories of great meals, of ambiance frozen in time and anecdotes that grow taller with the passing of the years.

I'm thinking here of Barry's, Gaston's, Belmondo's, Dooley's, Rio's and Coco's. Barry's succumbed to the developers, ringing in an era of much movement but little grace. This site suffered some hard years before

My favourite corner at Palmer's.

re-emerging as Dilozo's, a modern oasis of colour and light on the beach-front. Gaston's at Sunshine Beach, once all lawyer cane and laughter, is now Jean Luc Lapene's Cafe Des Amis. Belmondo's is now La Sabbia, and Dooley's is Roser's, Rio's is Rio's again and Coco's is still Coco's after all these years.

Some of our restaurants have stood the test of time, through changes of ownership, changes of chefs, the vagaries of human nature and the resort economy, and the fluctuations of food styles. The one constant in all of our great restaurants has been the kind of people who start them and operate them. More than most places of my experience, the industry is geared towards couples. Sometimes the restaurant breaks the relationship, other times it makes it. But in most cases the bond between the partners is the fire that sets these places alight.

The necessity to travel is also a common thread. Even the most established restaurateurs feel the need to fly the coop, recharge the batteries and find new inspirations. This has a lot to do with the fact that almost all of us came here as travellers, and the desire for new experiences does not diminish. The transient soul is alive and well, and this rootlessness adds another dimension to our restaurants. They are constantly evolving and reinventing themselves.

PALMER'S

In late 1984 I returned from a sojourn overseas with my new partner (later husband) Stef Fisher. We were bubbling with enthusiasm generated by our travels and our new relationship and started looking for a restaurant space on Hastings Street. The place that appealed most was Casa Majorca, a dark and dingy cafe at the Woods end of the street which also happened to be the smallest licensed premises in Queensland.

We would sit on the vacant block across the street and fantasise about the streetfront cafes and bars we had loved in Europe, and what could be done with Casa Majorca. There was no for sale sign in the window, but what isn't for sale in Noosa? Casa Majorca became the first Palmer's.

Palmer's was a success and we looked to expand. This was impossible in our little street frontage, but we found another site in the Ocean Breeze complex just up the road. Once again we gave it the long,

Me and main squeeze, Palmer's, late '80s.

BENGAL CURRY OF VEAL SHANKS

Serves 6

6 veal shanks, French trimmed
1 teasp chopped garlic
125ml/4^1/$_2$fl oz vegetable oil
450gm/1lb peeled baby onions
1 teasp salt
1 tablesp finely chopped
fresh ginger

1 teasp each ground turmeric,
coriander, cumin, cayenne
pepper, garam masala
450gm/1lb (4 medium sized)
potatoes, peeled and
quartered
1 tablesp sugar

Put shanks in tray, add turmeric, cumin, coriander, cayenne pepper, ginger and garlic. Mix well and set aside for 2 hours. Heat oil in large baking tray over medium flame. Let it smoke. Now scatter in sugar, and immediately put in onions. Stir and fry the onions until a rich brown in colour, add the shanks and brown for 10 minutes. Add potatoes and continue to brown for further 5 minutes.

Add salt and 500ml/18fl oz veal stock, bring to the boil, cover with foil and bake in 200°C/400°F oven for 2 hours, adding more stock if necessary.

Before serving stir the garam masala into the sauce, place shank over the dahl and spoon the sauce over.

Dahl

1 cup yellow split peas
1 onion, very finely diced
1 teasp curry powder
^{1}/$_2$ teasp salt

^{1}/$_4$ teasp turmeric
1 tablesp vegetable oil
300ml/10fl oz coconut milk

Saute onion with vegetable oil, turmeric and curry powder. Add split peas, cover with water and simmer until water has evaporated. Add coconut milk and salt and continue to simmer until dahl is soft and thick.

contemplative stare, sneaking into the shell of the former Ming Court late at night and imagining what we could do with it. Our dream was to create a signature restaurant in the Mediterranean style, while keeping what would come to be known affectionately as "Little Palmer's" (now the Aqua Bar) as a casual street-front trattoria. Our theory was that running two establishments would be twice as easy as one.

We took a lease on the premises and proceeded to raze it to the ground. We then spent three months working with our friend Peter Davies, a designer who had translated our vision to reality at Little Palmer's, creating a Mediterranean-influenced look that captured the colours and feel of Noosa, later to be marketed far and wide as Sandbag. At the new location we let Peter have his head.

As time went by we ran ourselves ragged trying to keep on top of the requirements of two places, and all too often we'd be at the wrong end of the street when we were needed. We decided to concentrate our efforts on what was fast becoming Noosa's favourite restaurant.

Top: Peter Davies in the shell that became Palmer's, 1987.

Above: Bengal curry of veal shanks.

Over the next seven years Palmer's went from strength to strength. It lost some of its early formality as it "wore in", and became a kind of home away from home for both locals and visitors. The food style changed from serious a la carte to a relaxed combination of platters of tapas and meals meant to be shared. Our kitchen staff changed as our chefs went off to start their own restaurants, but our signature style remained.

Our third chef, Vaughn Bligh, had worked for me at Rio's as a cheeky 16-year-old apprentice. When he'd finished his training he left to make his mark in Sydney and Europe, ultimately working as a consultant chef on Iain Hewitson's Last Aussie Fish Cafs along the east coast.

Above: Vaughn Bligh at work.

Below left: Pineapple brulee cheesecake (recipe page 128).

Below right: White chocolate panettone pudding.

The coolest place in town.

Below: Young Vaughn in the kitchen, 1987.

In 1993 the traveller in us became restless again, and we accepted an offer to establish a Palmer's at Irvin Rockman's Regency Hotel in Melbourne. We took Vaughn with us to head up the southern kitchen, but it was also his duty to make frequent trips back to Noosa to ensure quality control. On one of these trips, Vaughn and his partner Kevin Disher decided to make us an offer for Palmer's Noosa. Although we were somewhat reluctant to let our baby go, I was happy to sell to some one who understood the "Palmer's culture."

Vaughn's food philosophy is based strongly on the importance of visual impact and the flavour-packed first mouthful. He believes that once the customer is satisfied that the meal is up to his expectations, he can relax into the table conversation. At Palmer's Vaughn has put a lot of thought into his menu and presentation, accentuating the clean, simple and unfussed lines of modern minimalist dishes. His selection is driven by available produce rather than the market, and most dishes reflect his individuality and concern for nutrition. On the other hand, Vaughn loves a good pud, and produces wonderful desserts to tempt the most discerning and diet-conscious palates.

WHITE CHOCOLATE PANETTONE PUDDING WITH CHOCOLATE CREAM

1 Italian Panettone, bought from good deli
250ml/9fl oz milk
250ml/9fl oz cream
1 cup white chocolate buds
4 eggs and 1 egg yolk
$\frac{1}{2}$ cup sugar
$\frac{1}{2}$ teasp vanilla essence

Slice panettone into $\frac{1}{2}$cm/$\frac{1}{4}$inch slices and leave to dry slightly.

Heat milk, cream and chocolate buds until chocolate has dissolved.

Beat eggs with sugar and vanilla and pour hot chocolate cream mix over and stir until combined to make a custard.

In loaf tin place first layer of panettone, followed by custard mix. Repeat this process until tin is full.

Bake at 180°C/350°F for 30 minutes or until set. Leave to cool, unmould and slice. Place on serving plate and top with chocolate cream.

Dark Chocolate Cream

20gm/1oz dark chocolate buds
200ml/7fl oz cream

Slowly heat chocolate and cream together until chocolate has dissolved. Leave to cool slightly before serving.

ARTIS

Up on Noosa Hill opposite the pub, The Attic began life in the late 1960s. The distinctive A-frame cottage knew fame under Roy and Fay McKibbin and later under Mandy Holmes as Blueberry Hill. In 1993 it began its third incarnation as Artis.

Open and inviting, with its innovative style tumbling out of its foldback doors onto the cobbled courtyard, Francesca and David Horton's modern and lively establishment slowly conquered its growing pains and became a cornerstone of Noosa's food culture, winning the inaugural Noosa Good Food Awards in 1995.

The Hortons remodelled the interior so that Artis could become an art gallery and live music venue as well, in keeping with their philosophy that all three contributed to the quality of life. Art exhibitions and jazz evenings have become an important part of Artis, but the food and wine remains the driving force.

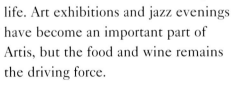

Above: Stock for red claw crayfish.

Left: Garry Flynn in the Artis kitchen.

Opposite page, top: David and Francesca Horton at Artis.

Opposite page, bottom: Red claw crayfish.

Chef Garry Flynn trained in Brisbane but cooking was neither an inherited skill nor an overriding passion until he travelled to Europe on a working holiday which kept him away for almost eight years. In England he worked in several London establishments and later ran a restaurant in the Cotswolds with wife Deborah, achieving a Michelin Guide mention, possibly the first Australian to do so in England.

Back in Australia, Garry lasted three days in a Gold Coast restaurant before he saw an ad for the position of chef at a new restaurant in Noosa. Being English, the Hortons immediately saw the breadth of his experience and hired him. The combination has been a winning one.

Garry's joy at Artis is to meld aspects of different ethnic cuisines with local produce – "never bastardising the original dish, but putting a different edge to it". He says his curiosity about cooking drives him on to investigate new combinations of flavours and to experiment. This, combined with his classical training, is the key to the distinctive Artis style.

The Hortons and Garry Flynn have also established a cooking school at the restaurant, and have devised a program of classes at different times of the year featuring Garry and some of Australia's renowned chefs.

RED CLAW CRAYFISH

(with grilled asparagus and crayfish jus)

12 large red claw crayfish, live (or fresh Moreton Bay bugs)
12 asparagus spears, blanched
100gm/3½oz fresh pasta, preferably linguine
2 tablesp fennel oil
4 teasp salmon caviar
4 teasp finely chopped chives

Cook crayfish in boiling water for 3 minutes and quickly place in iced water. Remove heads and twist the tails from their shells. Crack half the claws. Reserve the heads and half the claws for the sauce.

Sauce

crayfish heads and excess claws	6 golden shallots, sliced
1/4 cup diced carrot	1/4 cup diced leek
2 garlic cloves	2 button mushrooms
50ml/2fl oz brandy	400ml/14fl oz white wine
1 sprig thyme	1 sprig tarragon
2 star anise	1 teasp coriander seeds
1 teasp black peppercorns	1 lemon grass stalk, very finely
1 teasp chopped coriander root	chopped
1 teasp chopped ginger	4 tablesps butter

1x 450gm/1lb tin tomato, drained and pureed (or 8-10 medium
tomatoes, roasted, deseeded and pureed)

Saute the shallot, carrot, leek, garlic and mushrooms in 1 tablesp
of butter and 2 tablesp of peanut oil. Add the crayfish heads and
continue cooking for 1 minute.

Add brandy and cook it away then add the white wine, tomato,
tarragon. thyme, star anise, coriander seeds and peppercorns.
Simmer for 20 minutes. Strain through a fine sieve, pressing with
wooden spoon to remove all liquid.

Return to the saucepan and reduce by half. Add the lemon grass,
coriander root and ginger and simmer a further 5 minutes, then
pass through a fine sieve.

Cook the pasta al dente in lightly salted water.

Brush the asparagus spears with oil and grill them. Warm the
crayfish tails in a light fish or vegetable stock. Arrange the crayfish,
three tails to a serve, with the asparagus on warmed plates.

Quickly reheat the sauce, whisking in the butter which has been
cut into small cubes. Check seasoning. Spoon over the crayfish,
decorate the dish with several claws.

Moisten the pasta with the fennel oil, divide into four portions
and twist into a coil. Position the pasta on top. Garnish with
chives and caviar. Serve at once.

ANITA'S

The charming restaurant that greets you today bears little resemblance to the one Anita Bain and her husband Peter opened in Noosaville in 1988, but the Bains see constant evolution as part of the site's tradition.

Once a bait and tackle shop, the building was given a new facade in the 1960s when it became Dial-a-Bird, which despite what some people may have thought, was actually a take-away chicken shop.

The vision, energy and drive of the Bains has produced a restaurant that is a fine canvas for their hospitality skills and Anita's definitive food philosophy and style. Brisbane-born Anita attributes her instinctive love of cooking to her grandmother and remembers being highly incensed at kindergarten to find that there were no cooking classes available, typical of the strong will that has been apparent the whole time I have known her, and has stood her in good stead in this somewhat taxing industry.

Top: Anita.

Right: Anita's.

After leaving school, Anita travelled before returning to Noosa to be with her family. She started working for Pierre Otth at Coco's as a jill-of-all-trades, the beginning of a 12-year learning curve, picking up the tricks of the trade from Pierre and Luc Turschwell at a variety of their restaurants. She says now: "The Frenchmen taught me a lot about combinations of food and nutrition, which had always interested me. And, perhaps surprisingly, they were not the least bit chauvinistic."

Ajillo prawns.

Out on her own, Anita's first venture (in partnership with Dave Burgess) was a whimsical oasis in Noosa Junction she called Serendipity. The garden cafe, which had been Casa Ronaldo and the short-lived but spectacular Dook's Wine Bar, was a zen-influenced establishment that combined simple and healthy food with a touch of style.

Anita's is a reflection of all that Anita Bain has learned in 20 years of involvement in the local food industry, particularly her appreciation of "real food", which she defines as simple presentation of fresh ingredients – a plate of garfish from the river being just as enticing as a pink Atlantic salmon.

Chilli sorbet.

Anita says her food today is the culmination of two decades of soaking up the influences of the chefs she has worked with or admired, plus her own development as an innovator in the kitchen. For example, when Anita and Peter decided, after 16 years and two children together, to get married in New Mexico, she returned not only as Mrs Bain but with a great understanding of Santa Fe cuisine and its reliance on the subtle use of various types of chilli. This influence too has been absorbed into the Anita's menu.

Ajillo Prawns, Avocado and Grapefruit Salad

This dish is dedicated to the late Dani Harris. As a chef his enthusiasm, loyalty and energy knew no bounds.

Prawns

4 tablesp olive oil

2 tablesp butter

1kg/2$\frac{1}{4}$lb green prawns, shelled and deveined

4 cloves of garlic, peeled

1 tablesp minced garlic

2 tablesp sushi su vinegar

2 tablesp dry sherry

2 tablesp lime juice

$\frac{1}{2}$ teasp paprika

pinch chilli powder

Maldon salt and black pepper

125ml/4$\frac{1}{2}$fl veal stock, flavoured with bay leaf and thyme

2 tablesp chopped parsley

Heat a large saute pan or wok. Add olive oil. Add whole garlic over high heat. Add prawns, turn to seal. Pour olive oil out and add butter, minced garlic, paprika and chilli.

Saute for 1 minute, pour in vinegar and sherry. Add stock and season.

Cook until prawns are done, add parsley and lemon juice. Toss and serve with salad and sorbet.

Chilli Sorbet

1ltre/36fl oz water
3 cups castor sugar
zest of 4 lemons, finely chopped
2 cayenne chilli, split and seeds removed

Combine all ingredients in a saucepan, simmer for 8 minutes.
Remove from heat, add juice and cool. Churn and scoop.

Avocado and Grapefruit Salad

3 avocados, peeled and cubed
2 sweet grapefruit sliced
2 tablesp chives
salt and pepper
squeeze of lemon

Combine all ingredients and toss.

Durham's bait and tackle shop, now Anita's.

EDUARDO'S

A Noosa institution since it began life as Forty Baskets more than 20 years ago, this beachfront cafe has frequently had the threat of demolition hung over its head, and as we go to press it appears that its days are definitely numbered. After a period as an Indian BYO, Eduardo's was given its name by Eddie the Fisherman, a Noosa identity who sold to Lori and Ian Banks in 1990.

Under Lori Banks' zany direction, and partner Jean Luc Chaudet's European influence, Eddie's has enjoyed immense popularity with both visitors and locals, who delight in walking straight out of the surf and onto the covered deck for a fresh, light repast, like Eduardo's seafood curry.

Top: Position, position, position.

Top right: Jean Luc Chaudet.

Above: Crispy polenta with salad.

Right: Eduardo's on the inside.

Opposite: Eduardo's seafood curry.

One of the most interesting features of Eduardo's is the theatre of its working day. The cafe opens for breakfast at 7.30am and it is possible (not to mention enjoyable) to sit at a corner table for the next 16 hours and watch the changing cast of a typical Noosa day.

Lori and Jean Luc describe their fare as Mediterranean with an Asian influence.

EDUARDO'S THAI STYLE SEAFOOD CURRY

Serves 1

350gm/12oz mixed fresh seafood
150ml/5fl oz coconut milk
4 stalks of fresh coriander
1 fresh tomato, chopped
splash of fish sauce
1 teasp-1 tablesp curry paste, according to taste
condiments, such as coconut covered, sliced banana
and pickled cucumber

Heat a frying pan, add 2 tablesp peanut oil. Add the curry paste and fry for 2 minutes.

Place remaining ingredients in pan, cover with coconut milk and simmer until cooked.

Serve with jasmine rice and condiments.

Eduardo's Crisp Polenta With A Salad Of Marinated Onion, Sun-dried Tomato And Shaved Parmesan

For the Polenta

Boil 1ltre/36fl oz of water in a heavy saucepan. Once boiled remove from heat and slowly whisk in 250gm/9oz of polenta. Cover and simmer for 45 minutes over a very low heat.

Remove from heat and whilst still hot mix through 120gm/4½oz of hard butter, 50gm/2oz of grated parmesan cheese and season to taste.

Pour mix onto flat tray and smooth out until 2.5cm/1inch thick. Allow to cool.

Salad

Marinate half a Spanish onion in balsamic vinegar for 2 hours.

Make composite salad with marinated onion, finely sliced, sundried tomatoes, cherry tomatoes, kalamata olives and mesclun mix. Dress with your favourite dressing.

Cut polenta into fingers and using a non-stick frying pan and a little oil, fry each finger until golden brown.

Place over salad and top with shaved parmesan cheese.

LA PLAGE

Created by Pierre and Colette Otth, this Hastings Street restaurant has been a culinary landmark for more than 10 years. Under the direction of Colette Otth, the restaurant developed an arts focus, hosting first exhibitions for many local artists.

The design of the restaurant is a perfect example of a flow-through from inside to out, with pedestrian traffic seeming to move through the middle of the restaurant. One of my fondest memories of La Plage is during an early Hastings Street Festival, when Pierre set up his brazier on the footpath and filled the street with the irresistible smell of baby octopus char-grilling. To me, it seemed this is the way life in Noosa should be.

Today the restaurant is owned and operated by the Kinnear and Parry families, and Lucinda Kinnear is chef. Lucinda has continued La Plage's tradition of presenting stylish modern cuisine.

COCO'S

Coco's is one of the all-time survivors. It has retained its name and glorious position for more than three decades since it began as Coco's Palm Garden Cafe; from tea-room to take-away to cafe, through more facelifts than any woman I have ever known.

Today it is a well-appointed licensed restaurant with a canopy-covered all-weather garden offering spectacular views across Laguna Bay to Double Island Point. It offers a warm welcome and a much-needed cold drink to walkers, joggers and birdwatchers as they fall out of the National Park.

Owners Nicolas and Carina Romer took over at the beginning of 1989 and have continued the tradition established by Pierre Otth of serving light, innovative fare.

Above: Coco's courtyard.

Opposite: La Plage and caille du chef.

Right: tapas platter.

La Plage
Caille du Chef

Serves 6

6 boned large quail
1 bunch rocket   1 large gold sweet potato

Marinade

1 tablesp finely chopped
fresh ginger
¼ cup sweet soy sauce
¼ cup virgin olive oil

1 teasp chopped garlic
¼ cup fresh coriander
2 fresh birdseye chillies,
chopped

Dressing

¼ cup white wine vinegar
1 cup virgin olive oil
¼ cup fresh coriander

¼ cup roasted unsalted
cashew nuts
1 teasp Dijon mustard

salt and pepper to taste
roasted chopped cashew nuts and red chilli flower to garnish

Mix all ingredients of marinade together and add quail. Marinate for at least 24 hours.

Peel and slice rounds of gold sweet potato about ½cm/¼inch thick. Bake in 180°C/350°F oven with a little olive oil, for 20 minutes.

Put vinegar, cashew nuts, coriander, mustard, salt, pepper and garlic in a food processor and blend until combined. Slowly add olive oil while mixing.

Seal the quail on a chargrill or barbecue, and finish off in the oven for about 10 minutes at 180°C/350°F.

To assemble, put enough dressing on a large plate to cover it thinly and evenly. Place sweet potato in the centre of the plate. Put a small handful of rocket on top and arrange the quail as desired and garnish.

COCO'S TAPAS

These dishes are served with such tastes as salmon and tofu nori rolls, golden cuttlefish and crisp spring rolls.

Shiu Mai
(Steamed Dumplings)

500gm/18oz minced chicken or pork
250gm/9oz green prawn meat, finely chopped
10 water chestnuts, finely chopped
8 dried shitake mushrooms, soaked 30 minutes in hot water,
drain, discard stems and chop finely
1 cup finely chopped Chinese cabbage
$1\frac{1}{2}$ teasp sesame oil
2 tablesps light soy
$\frac{1}{2}$ tablesp sugar
1 packet wonton wrappers

Combine all ingredients except wonton wrappers. Mix thoroughly and squeeze through fingers until sticky. Refrigerate 30 minutes. Put heaped teaspoons of mixture on each wonton wrapper and gather around filling. Arrange dumplings on lightly oiled steamer, cover, place over rapidly boiling water and steam for 12 minutes.

Lemon Peppered Kangaroo

500gm/18oz Kangaroo fillet
lemon pepper seasoning

Roll kangaroo fillet in lemon pepper. Oil hot-plate. Cook on medium-high heat for 4 minutes. Turn and cook 3 minutes other side or until rare. Remove from heat and leave 10 minutes before slicing.

LINDONI'S

New Zealand-born Alan and Pam Lindon started Lindoni's in 1989, creating Noosa's first serious Italian restaurant. Lindoni's presents Italian cuisine from all regions but specialises in the lighter southern style from regions not dissimilar to our own, such as Positano, Amalfi and Capri.

The restaurant exudes the atmosphere of an Italian villa, decorated inside with mementos of the Lindons' annual visit to Italy. The courtyard, under one large white umbrella, is a place to see and be seen, the perfect place to view the Hastings Street shuffle.

Lindoni's cotoletta di vitello.

THE JETTY

Another old-timer, this Boreen Point lake-front restaurant has been owned and operated by Edi Brunetti and Judy Walter since the early 1980s. The Jetty is a 15-minute drive from Noosa, or better still, an hour's boat trip up the beautiful Noosa River. Edi, an Italian gentleman of the old style, greets diners with a glass of wine, many words of wisdom and always superb hospitality.

The set menu consists of fresh, spontaneous home-style dishes created by chef Judy and brought to the table in groaning platters to share. I have never seen anyone leave The Jetty hungry – often diners leave sated on Judy's specialities like whole baked fish or leg of lamb.

Banana meringue roulade.

Lindoni's Cotoletta di Vitello

Serves 4

4 veal cutlets, approximately 240gm/9oz each
3 small zucchini   4 yellow squash
1 red capsicum   1 green capsicum
$\frac{1}{2}$ onion   8 button mushrooms
200ml/7fl oz reduced veal stock   100ml/4fl oz Frascati
30 sage leaves   6 medium potatoes
50ml/2fl oz milk   2 tablesp butter
3 tablesp olive oil
$\frac{1}{3}$ cup freshly ground parmesan cheese

Rub zucchini and squash lightly with olive oil, cook on chargrill and set aside.

Roast capsicums under hot grill and sweat in a plastic bag to release skins. Cut into batons.

Chargrill mushrooms and onion pieces.

Peel and cut potatoes. Boil in salted water, drain when cooked. Mash with milk, butter, olive oil and parmesan. Keep warm.

Shallow fry sage leaves for about 30 seconds. Drain.

Heat a heavy fry pan, seal veal cutlets and then finish on the chargrill.

Deglaze pan with Frascati. Reduce by $\frac{2}{3}$, add veal stock and reduce until a coating consistency. Add a knob of butter and a little chopped sage.

Place mashed potatoes in the centre of the plate, top with the grilled vegetables and the cutlet.

Pour sauce over and top with fried sage leaves.

THE JETTY BANANA MERINGUE ROULADE WITH PASSIONFRUIT CREAM

6 egg whites	a pinch of salt
300gm/10oz castor sugar	1 teasp cornflour
1 teasp vinegar	1 teasp vanilla essence
sweetened whipped cream	3 ripe bananas

sifted icing sugar and shredded coconut

passionfruit cream

Pre-heat the oven to 160°C/310°F. Line a 24 x 32cm (10 x 12inch) tin with baking paper. Beat the egg whites with the pinch of salt until stiff peaks form. Add the sugar gradually while still beating. The mixture should be thick and glossy. Fold in the vanilla, vinegar and cornflour. Spread the meringue into the tin evenly and bake for 20 minutes. Cool in the tin for a few minutes before turning out onto a sheet of baking paper that has been dusted with icing sugar and shredded coconut. When the meringue has cooled, spread with the whipped cream and sliced bananas. Roll up carefully, using the paper to get the roulade shape. Refrigerate until required.

Passionfruit Cream

150ml/5fl oz passionfruit juice	8 large egg yolks
100gm/3$\frac{1}{2}$oz castor sugar	300ml/10fl oz cream

Whisk all ingredients together in a bowl. Place bowl over pan of boiling water and cook until it reaches the consistency of a thick custard. Pass through a sieve if necessary, cover with clingwrap and refrigerate.

To serve, spoon some passionfruit cream onto the plate and place a slice of roulade on top. Drizzle with passionfruit pulp and dust with icing sugar.

THE NEW BREED

THE TERM "NEW BREED" refers to an attitude, rather than to newcomers to town. Most of the restaurants and cafes I have featured are in fact operated by people who have cut their teeth elsewhere, learned the nuances of Noosa and struck out in the 1990s to create places that reflect their individuality. All but one are off Hastings Street, indicative of 1990s economic realities. Positions away from the passing trade mean that they have to be confident in what they are doing, and this shows through in their approach to the food, design and styling of their restaurants.

SALTWATER

Owners Steve and Lisa Cross had many years of living in Noosa, and one successful restaurant endeavour behind them when they decided to leap onto the smallest site on Hastings Street and create what was originally intended to be an upmarket fish and chip shop.

Eschewing designers, the Crosses consulted with local craftsmen and builders on the best use of their small and sharply-angled site. They built the downstairs shop around existing trees, then, realising the potential of the upper level, they decided to create a cafe. Five metres wide by 17.5 metres long, the space looks out over a vista of Noosa street life, the colourful shutters and awnings evocative of Greece or Turkey.

Downstairs the shop is dominated by the "toadstool" tables and glass display counter, featuring a mouth-watering array of fresh local mud crabs, prawns, oysters and Saltwater's small produce line, which includes pickles and sauces to complement the seafood.

The Crosses like to serve most of their seafood dishes unadorned except for the simplest Mediterranean or Asian touches, such as Buderim ginger and sweet soy sauce. They believe that the quality of the cooking is everything, and while they encourage customers to try their versions of such local fish as tailor and mullet, Saltwater's most popular dish is their superb rendition of traditional fish and chips. Steve Cross himself says that he prefers to eat the fish of the region. While in Adelaide he would eat King George whiting and in Melbourne a plate of black mussels, in Noosa he can't go past a North Shore tailor.

The Crosses are very interested in wine and have developed ties with several leading and boutique wineries to put together one of Noosa's more interesting wine lists.

SUMMER CARAMELISED TOMATO TART

12 firm ripe Roma tomatoes	12 golden eschallot bulbs
extra virgin olive oil	balsamic vinegar
white sugar	Webber barbecue
Cheat's Puff Pastry	1 cup plain flour
soda or sparkling mineral water	100gm/3$\frac{1}{2}$oz butter

Set the Webber to heat on "indirect" cooking.

Halve the tomatoes lengthwise and set them, cut side up, on a piece of strong Alfoil with the sides turned up to make a circle. Sprinkle with about a teasp of sugar, drizzle with oil and then be fairly liberal with splashing balsamic vinegar over the lot.

Slide this onto the roasting rack of the Webber and allow to "semi-dry" for 45 minutes.

Wrap the unpeeled golden eschallots in another piece of foil and slip these in for 15 minutes. After a total of 1 hour, remove both. Allow the eschallots to cool before peeling.

The tomato foil will have a black layer of caramelised balsamic. Turn the tomatoes over and push the peeled eschallots into the spaces. Dissolve half a cup of sugar in as little water as possible in a small saucepan, over medium heat. Continue to cook until the syrup just starts to turn golden. Pour over the tomatoes.

Pastry

Melt the butter and allow to return to tepid, but still liquid.

Tip the flour into a bowl. Mix in enough soda water to make a soft dough. Quickly knead together on floured marble and roll out immediately into a circle.

Brush with as much butter as possible and cut into 8 triangles. Layer these one on top of the other and roll up in plastic wrap. Refrigerate the pastry while the tomatoes are finishing otherwise it gets too hard to roll out.

To top the tart, just roll into a circle and arrange over the top of the tomatoes.

Brush with the remaining butter and bake, this time in a normal oven, for about 30 minutes at 180°C/350°F or until the pastry is golden brown.

Allow to rest for 10 minutes before inverting onto a serving plate.

The pastry isn't flaky like puff, but when you cut it you do see the results of using a naan-type recipe and the crunchy texture is a great foil for the meltingly soft tomatoes.

CHILLI JAM CAFE

Wollongong-born Paul Blain trained as a chef in a variety of Sydney restaurants and then furthered his career in South East Asia and at Sydney's Darley Street Thai. This background, plus his hands-on passion for cooking have come together to win him widespread acclaim for the innate artistry of his work at Chilli Jam Cafe.

Popping up to Noosa for a few days R & R from the heavy baggage of the Sydney restaurant life, Paul saw a professional and lifestyle

Above: Paul Blain grinding fresh spices.

Right: Chilli Jam's bug curry.

opportunity and was back to stay a few weeks later. He worked in some one else's restaurant until he found a space above a convenience store in Noosaville which had a long and undistinguished track record as a restaurant venue, and was considered by many to be a "dog". For Paul, it represented a functional and affordable space overlooking the river, and he knew he could make it succeed.

Paul prides himself on the innovations he employs, and his fear of routine creeping into his food means that whenever Chilli Jam is open, Paul is in the kitchen. From an authentic Thai food base, in Noosa Paul's cooking has evolved into a hybrid of styles from different Thai regions and the influence of local produce and market demand. Over two years he has developed a close working relationship with local growers, ensuring a ready supply of such ingredients as fresh peppercorns, cardamon, green pawpaws, holy basil and kaffir lime leaves. Paul also speaks enthusiastically about the prospects of pippies, wild cockles, Lake Doonella skate and bugs from Fraser Island, but his adventurous streak is tempered by the restrictions of the Fish Management Authority.

Gaeng Bama Hoi Pla (Yellow Curry Of Fraser Island Bugs)

This is a light but very flavoursome curry suitable for fish and shellfish, not taking the flavour away from the seafood, but adding to its richness.

Serves 2

Curry Paste

$1/4$ cup ginger, peeled and chopped
$1/2$ cup garlic
$1/2$ cup red shallots
2 tablesp coriander seeds, roasted and ground

1 tablesp chilli powder, roasted
1 tablesp turmeric
$\frac{1}{2}$ teasp sea salt

Combine all the above ingredients and blend in a food processor to a smooth paste.

3-4 Fraser Island bugs
2-4 long red chillies
6-8 Kaffir lime leaves
1-2 ripe tomatoes
6-8 small slivers of butternut pumpkin
1 cup plucked Thai basil
1 stick of lemon grass
4 tablesp safflower oil
$\frac{1}{2}$ tablesp palm sugar
1 tablesp fish sauce
400ml/14fl oz coconut cream

In a saucepan large enough to house the bugs, place the oil and bring to a medium heat.

Add the curry paste and fry, stirring to prevent sticking.

Add the pumpkin, chillies, lime leaves, and lemon grass stick, stir.

Add the palm sugar and allow to caramelise a little, then add the fish sauce and deglaze the pan.

Add the coconut cream, the bugs, cut side face down, and the tomatoes. Allow to simmer slowly to cook the bugs, 2-4 minutes, depending on the size.

Finally when the ingredients are cooked and the curry is slightly thicker, add the basil and serve immediately.

Garnish with sprigs of coriander. Best served with steamed, jasmine scented rice.

FILLIGAN'S

In the cottage that once housed the Munna Point general store, Peter Gilligan created Hot Gillie's, a funky Mexican BYO beloved of the campers across the road. After five years of beans, tequila and cocoracha, Peter and partner Stevie ("Wonder") McKernan parted company and Hot Gillie's belatedly entered the '90s with a complete makeover (with the help of design guru Peter Davies) and re-emerged as Filligan's.

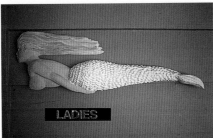

Above: Jamaican goat curry.

Below right: Filligan's Dave Burgess.

The "Fill" of the new name was founding chef Phil Mitchell, who helped set the style for this unpretentious riverside eatery, which soon became a favoured hang-out for locals as well as holiday-makers in the know.

Peter's association with Noosa goes back to the early '70s when he wore a long-sleeved Hawaiian shirt under a velvet vest as a waiter at the Green Cherry (now the Sheraton Noosa Resort). Later, when he became a restaurateur in his own right, I lived next door. In fact, when Clover my dog died, we buried her under a tree at my place and later Peter transplanted it to his back yard. That poincettia now forms the entrance to Filligan's backyard gazebo.

Today the restaurant has a homely feel. You can wander through as if it were your own home, from street-side tables through the restaurant proper to the Balinese-influenced back garden. Peter encourages this informality and impromptu parties are a regular occurrence, usually encouraged by his staff of veteran Noosa waiters, most of whom are called Dave.

Filligan's food is described in their menu as "modern alternative cuisine", and I wouldn't argue with that. Phil Mitchell, who has now moved on to new challenges, created the signature dish, scorched cuttlefish. (See The Faces for a recipe.) The menu makes for easy listening, touched with the mood of tropical places, quirky and well-crafted dishes. Peter and the Daves have a wealth of experience in pairing wines with food, and Filligan's list is both seductive and affordable.

Peter Gilligan.

JAMAICAN GOAT CURRY

1kg/2¼lb lean diced goat	1 medium onion
4 shallots	2 cloves garlic, crushed

½ red capsicum and ½ green capsicum, seeded and diced
into 1 x 1cm/½ x ½inch pieces

3 sprigs fresh thyme	2 tablesp curry powder
2 teasp cumin	½ teasp turmeric
1 teasp garam masala	2 teasp celery salt
1ltre/36fl oz approx veal stock	1 medium potato

4 celery leaves, roughly chopped for garnish

Combine garlic, chopped thyme, curry powder, cumin, turmeric, garam masala and celery salt. Mix into diced goat, cover and sit refrigerated for at least 24 hours.

Heat 200ml/7fl oz olive oil and saute until browned with onion and shallots. Add stock and simmer for 20 minutes.

Add diced potato and simmer until tender.

Add capsicum and when tender serve garnished with chopped celery leaves.

MANGO AND LIME CHUTNEY

½ cup sugar	1 cup cider vinegar
200gm/7oz lime pickle	1½kg/3½lb mango flesh

Reduce sugar and vinegar until a syrup.

Add lime pickle and stir until well combined.

Add mango flesh and simmer, approximately 15 minutes.

SOLEIL

More than any of the European chefs who have found their way to Noosa, Patrick Landelle was trained in the classic way of the Old World, even to the point of receiving his game meat as carcasses needing to be skinned, cleaned, hung and cut. These and the other time-neglected skills of the classic kitchen have given him a very different approach to his work.

Patrick trained in Alsace, then worked as a commis in Switzerland and Austria. Later he travelled to South Africa and set up a restaurant called Backstage in Cape Town. Appropriately, he met Rayne, an English girl working in theatre, and together they travelled to Scandinavia in search of work and adventure. In Norway one freezing night they sat up in bed together, sipping on a bottle of Bailey's Irish Cream to sustain body heat, and decided that a warmer climate beckoned. They chose Australia.

Above left: Mediterranean octopus tart. *Above: Lamb loin in miso.*

In Noosa, Patrick took a job cooking for Steve Cross at Touché Restaurant, and later went with the Crosses to Saltwater. Casting about for a venture of his own, Patrick found a site perfectly positioned at Sunshine Beach. He and Rayne knew it had to be called Soleil (French for "sun"), representing the choice they had made when they left Norway.

Patrick's vision for his own restaurant was of a beach kiosk with style. He commissioned architect Will Franklin to design an open, friendly space of curves, colour and maximum ocean views. Indeed, even Patrick's open kitchen affords a view to the blue Pacific. Patrick considers the view and the direct sunlight important adjuncts to the food he cooks, helping to create an energy that fires up both cook and customers.

The Soleil menu is built around entree portions of "feel-good" food. The food philosophy is that their holidaymaker clientele want to taste a variety of smaller portions, giving them a feel for what Soleil has to offer.

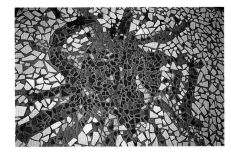

Mediterranean Tartlets Of Chargrilled Octopus With Black Olive Dressing

Serves 6

Shortcrust pastry pre-prepared, enough to line 6 small cases
4 garlic cloves, smashed   100ml/4fl oz olive oil
2 eggplants, sliced   2 zucchini, sliced
2 red onions, sliced   fresh basil
2 red and 1 green capsicum, cut lengthwise into 6 strips
1 leek, sliced and cleaned
600gm/1¼lb octopus

Mix together above ingredients (apart from pastry and octopus) and add salt and pepper to taste, then chargrill.

Cook octopus in boiling water for 2 minutes then plunge into ice-cold water. When cold, thread onto skewers, allowing 2 per person, then chargrill, brushed with oil.

Black Olive Dressing

200gm/7oz black olives, stoneless
½ cup virgin olive oil
¼ cup balsamic vinegar   1 onion chopped
1 tablesp French mustard   5 cloves of garlic, crushed
salt and pepper   Blend together.

To assemble tart, fill pastry cases with charred vegetables, place charred skewers of octopus on top, then drizzle with black olive dressing. Garnish with fresh basil.

LAMB LOIN IN MISO WITH JERUSALEM ARTICHOKE

Serves 6

3 lamb loins, cut in half
1 pkt dark miso
600gm/1¼lb Jerusalem artichokes, cleaned and blanched
500ml/20fl oz demi glace
100ml/4fl oz sherry
black pepper and salt
100gm/3½oz butter
100ml/4fl oz sweet soy sauce

Mix miso and sherry with pepper and marinate lamb loins for at least 6 hours.

Slice Jerusalem artichokes then panfry with butter and set aside.
Chargrill the lamb loins according to taste.

Mix demi glace and sweet soy and reduce until sauce coats the back of a spoon.

Assemble all on a plate by placing lamb on top of artichokes, drizzling with sauce and garnishing with spring onions.

Patrick Landelle and son.

THE SPIRIT HOUSE

Peter and Helen Brierty ran Misty's of Montville for many years until the wanderlust took a grip on them and they began extended travels in Thailand. The Thai culture became a passion and when they returned to Australia they began the search for a place to recreate it in some way.

On a plot of land at Yandina, south west of Noosa, they created a Thai-style garden which they opened to the public. This led to a demand that they sell some of the plants on display, and Avant

Right: Crispy seafood noodle balls in the fryer.

CRISPY FRIED SEAFOOD NOODLE BALLS

200gm/7oz cooked Chinese egg noodles - cut into pieces
200gm/7oz chopped prawns
200gm7oz chopped squid
1 dessertsp Sambal Oelek
1 dessertsp ginger, finely chopped
1 red onion, finely sliced
$\frac{1}{2}$ cup chopped coriander, leaves and stems
3 eggs
$\frac{1}{2}$ cup plain flour
splash of fish sauce
vegetable oil for deep frying

Combine all the ingredients.

Form into rough balls, walnut-sized (any bigger and they become doughy in the middle).

Heat oil in wok or deep frying pan (about 5cm/2inch deep), until just smoking.

Deep fry until golden brown, drain on kitchen paper.

Serve with sweet chilli sauce.

Sweet Chilli Sauce

1 cup coconut vinegar
2 cups white sugar
1 tablesp garlic, crushed
1 tablesp Sambal Oelek

Combine all ingredients in saucepan, bring to the boil, then simmer for 2 minutes. Cool and store in clean jar. Use as a dipping sauce.

Gardens became their plant nursery, and later a hydroponic farm supplying local restaurants and food outlets. The natural progression was to a restaurant within the grounds, offering visitors a total Thai experience. The vision for the Spirit House took a long time and a lot of hard work to come to fruition, but it was worth it. Today, the visitor meanders through garden paths, past lily-fringed ponds to a man-made lake, upon one bank of which is an eating pavilion with covered tables hidden in the foliage along the adjacent bank. Ducks glide, birds sing, the colours consume you, everything is beautiful. And four years earlier, there was nothing here.

Chef Annette Fear had travelled widely in South East Asia before returning to Australia and working with Eduardo's chef Di Heaney, who she credits with helping to blend her own cooking style with the Noosa influences. When she met up with Helen and Peter, both parties realised that their backgrounds were complementary, and the creation of the Spirit House simply flowed.

Annette describes her cooking as "clean and fragrant", with a great emphasis on the preparation and selection of ingredients. She also makes good use of the available fresh fruits of the region. On one visit I was bowled over by a jug of watermelon juice, completely unadorned by vodka, the perfect complement to the green papaya salad with sweet pork.

Chef Annette Fear.

THE FACES

FACES BELONG on both sides of our tables. There are the regulars who appear through the door maybe once a week; there are the customers who come maybe once each holiday season, but they keep coming year after year, and they seek you out at whichever establishment you're at. Then there are the familar faces on our side of the table; the chefs, waiters, bar staff, owners and operators who seem to have been in Noosa forever. I can think of so many people - well-known and not so - who have contributed to our food culture, breathing life into many a venture with style, humour and hard work. There is only room within these pages to celebrate a few, but I hope they represent the spirit of many.

Edi Brunetti, with chef Judy Walter, runs The Jetty Restaurant at Boreen Point on the Lake Cootharabah shore. A Noosa resident for more than 20 years, he has had such restaurants and night spots as Rio's and the Beach Chalet, but it is at The Jetty that he has put his own Italianate stamp on Noosa style. Hospitality is Edi's forte, everything done in the grand manner, including flourishing service, much hand-kissing and joke-telling. In fact, Edi is perhaps one of the best raconteurs in town. Take time to savour the accent. Edi loves life, and everyone loves Edi.

Edi's Pippies

Edi believes that the humble eugarie is the perfect complement to good wine and conversation. Late one night, watching the moon rise over Laguna Bay, he told me his technique:

"Take a bucket full of pippies and cover with fresh water, stand 24 hours (to drain out the sand).

Put a wide, heavy-based pan on a high heat.

Put in a little light olive oil, some finely chopped garlic, the pippies, a pinch of black pepper, a good splash of white wine and a handful of chopped parsley. (Keep another handful of chopped parsley for later.)

Have ready a big platter and as the pippies open, transfer them to the platter. When they are all open (conventional wisdom says don't eat the unopened ones, but both Edi and I do!) strain the juice through a fine sieve, pour over the pippies and add the rest of the parsley.

Eat with much gusto, white wine, crusty bread, flourishing of arms and deep and meaningful conversation."

PHIL MITCHELL'S SCORCHED CUTTLEFISH

1kg/2$\frac{1}{4}$ cuttlefish, skinned and cleaned
extra virgin olive oil
Marinade:
1 cup sesame oil
2 teasp Sambal Oelek
2 large pieces of fresh ginger, peeled and grated
4 cloves of garlic, skinned. smashed and chopped to a paste
1 bunch of coriander, washed, shaken and small stems and leaves,
roughly chopped
4 tablesp fish sauce
juice and zest of 2 limes

Place cleaned cuttlefish on chopping board.

Take sharp knife and make angled horizontal and vertical incisions and cut into diagonal pieces about 6cm long.

Mix all marinade ingredients together in a steel bowl.

Place cuttlefish in marinade and toss to coat well. Cover with cling wrap and place in refrigerator for 2 hours to allow the flavours and cuttlefish to marry.

Place a cast iron skillet on high burner and drizzle with a little extra virgin olive oil.

Bring pan to near smoking point and carefully place cuttlefish skin side down, (that is the scored side) and sear for a couple of minutes and turn once.

The result should have a slightly opaque centre to ensure a moist and succulent taste.

Serve at once with your favourite sweet chilli sauce, a mayonnaise with coriander leaves blended through and a mesclun salad.

Phil Mitchell is a pretty tall chap, even for an Englishman; he has to bend further over his stoves than most of us, which to me indicates that he really loves his craft.

Trained in the classical hotel kitchens of London, Phil honed his talents in Europe and, always looking for adventure, found himself in Australia on a working holiday. After a short stint in Sydney he was off once again, this time to Morocco, but there Phil found he had fallen in love...with Australia. He migrated and worked first at Bedarra Island resort before coming south. In Noosa he discovered Palmer's and we got to talking after dinner, which soon led to a three-and-a-half year working liaison which saw us scale great plates.

In the great Noosa tradition, Phil decided the time had come to branch out on his own, which he did with another fine chef - their restaurant, appropriately enough, was called Two Chefs. Time out after this venture saw him into a couple of consultancies before establishing Filligan's with owner Peter Gilligan. Ever footloose, Phil is now freelancing again.

Top: Black Sambucca flumery.

Above: Scorched cuttlefish

PHIL MITCHELL'S BLACK SAMBUCCA FLUMMERY

The dictionary defines flummery as: a nonsense, idle chit-chat or something created from eggs, milk and flour. Phil Mitchell remembers it as a childhood taste sensation.

3 farm fresh eggs, whole   2 egg yolks
125gm/4$\frac{1}{2}$oz castor sugar   10gm/$\frac{1}{2}$oz plain white flour
250ml/9fl oz milk   250ml/9fl oz cream, thickened
20ml/$\frac{3}{4}$fl oz black Sambucca

Break eggs and with the yolks, castor sugar and flour place in a clean stainless steel bowl and whisk until ribbon stage is reached, when the whisk is lifted and the eggs and sugar leave a trail.

Bring the cream and milk to the boil and along with the Sambucca, pour over the beaten eggs, stirring with a wooden spoon. Strain the mixture into a pouring jug.

Divide the mixture between 6 dariole moulds and sit them in a high-sided baking tin. Add warm water to about $\frac{2}{3}$ of the way up the moulds. Cover with tin foil and bake in pre-heated oven (180°C/350°F to 200°C/400°F) for 30 to 35 minutes.

To test if the flummeries are ready, gently lift a corner of the tin foil,(roll back with caution as the steam trapped will be released). Agitate one of the moulds to test that the mixture seems firm.

Remove from the oven and place on a cooling tray.

Refrigerate for 2 hours. Remove from the moulds, and top-side up, sprinkle liberally with sugar and glaze under pre-heated grill, or with a blow torch.

Serve on white plate splashed with black Sambucca and garnish with thin slices of liquorice (straws).

KONING'S DEATH BY CHOCOLATE CAKE

Makes 2 32cm/12inch long terrine tins
300gm/14oz dark chocolate buttons
1$\frac{1}{2}$ cups of castor sugar
2 tablesp strong black coffee
10 eggs, separated

Melt chocolate and coffee in microwave on medium heat –
or over saucepan of boiling water.

Beat in egg yolks with a fork.

Whisk egg whites until stiff and gradually add the sugar,
whisking continually until mixture has a satiny finish.

Fold in chocolate mixture.

Put mixture into 2 lamington trays, 30cm/12inch x 25cm/10inch,
lined with greaseproof paper, and bake at 180°C/350°F for
45 minutes

Ganache

1$\frac{1}{2}$kg/3$\frac{1}{2}$lb dark chocolate buttons
900ml/32fl oz cream
1 dessertsp coffee powder

Melt all the ingredients together and stir until well combined.

To assemble cake, first line terrine tins with greaseproof paper.
Turn out chocolate cakes when cool and cut each one into three
pieces, lengthwise.

Starting with ganache, alternate layers of ganache and cake
finishing with a cake layer. Repeat process in the second tin.

Refrigerate overnight. Turn out, slice and serve.

John and Sue Koning.

When the backpackers took over Airlie Beach in the late 1970s, Susie and John Koning decided the time was right to look for greener pastures. They found Noosa and began to work front of house in the emerging restaurant scene, which then included Annabelle's, The Wharf and Pierre's at the Noosa International.

Preferring to live out of town on acreage, the Konings started experimenting with a baby market garden and were soon supplying the kitchen of their own first establishment, the Eumundi Teahouse. They grew such exotics as cherry tomatoes, mignonette lettuce and herbs. They incubated their own eggs and Susie ground her own flour.

This dual love of gardens and restaurants led them to take over Picnics at Fairhill, the region's first restaurant within a nursery. In the early '90s they moved again, this time to build and establish Eats At Eumundi, a stylish cafe deli which soon became a magnet for the market crowd. The next and current challenge for the Konings was to resuscitate an old Queenslander on the edge of a spectacular rainforest and establish Harry's On Buderim, an instant success.

Sydney-born Di Heaney is an Asiaphile. She takes off for more adventures in Burma, Borneo and Thailand but something keeps

Above: Death by chocolate cake.

Right: Red curry of spatchcock.

Below: Di Heaney.

DI HEANEY'S RED CURRY OF SPATCHCOCK

Serves 1

1 spatchcock
1 tablesp red curry paste
1 cup coconut milk (water down if you prefer it not so rich)
2 kaffir lime leaves
2 10cm/4inch sticks of lemon grass (root end)
1 tablesp of oil
whole red chillies – to taste

Chop the backbone out of the spatchcock, cut in half then quarters.

Heat the oil in a frying pan and sear the spatchcock pieces, add the curry paste and coat the spatchcock.

Fry for a minute then add the coconut milk, lime leaves, lemon grass and chillies. Cook on medium heat until the spatchcock is cooked through and tender.

The sauce should be a little bit soupy.

A superb dish, serve with freshly cooked Thai jasmine rice.

Cooking time approx 20 minutes.

dragging her back to Noosa. A natural talent in the kitchen, she has helped establish Michel's at Netanya, Eduardo's and Dilozo's. (She was the "Di" part.)

After her most recent return from Asia, Di took over a chicken shop in Noosa Junction, but after watching too many chicken on the spit, Di had a spit, pulled out the rotisserie and replaced it with her own imported Burmese furniture, wooden horses and large comfortable chairs. Enter Rangoon Cafe, where Di puts her Asian influences to work, creating light, tasty and wholesome dishes in a slightly haphazard, totally Di way.

The first of the Jean Lucs to come to attention in Noosa, Jean Luc Lapene burst onto the scene in the late 1970s. His Gallic brashness concealed a shy and sensitive nature, but he always put maximum energy into every project he undertook. He moved from Roy McKibbon's Attic to Luc Turschwell's Belmondo's to my Rio's.

After a stint at the oh-so-French Cafe Le Monde on Hastings Street, Jean Luc moved to the quieter environs of Sunshine Beach to establish Cafe Des Amis, where he presides over a chaotically casual bar beloved of locals.

Jean Luc at Cafe Des Amis.

THE STAGE

THERE HAS ALWAYS BEEN a great deal of pride taken in the presentation of the restaurants and cafes of Noosa. Early on this showed more in themed venues or simple, rustic affairs, the design often dictated by budget, or lack of it.

Dooley's, for example, being an Irish seafood establishment, was all green and white checks; Barry's, being sophisticated, was all red plush booths; Belmondo's had simple blue and white touches in the Mediterranean style; and Forty Baskets (where Eduardo's is now) had the obligatory hanging nets and glass floats. As our restaurants developed

---

in stature and reputation and growing custom gave us more funds, we started to use more design talent (much of it local) and started to attract the notice of national magazines.

Soon Noosa's restaurants and cafes had developed a reputation for style as well as food, and although this style has constantly evolved, its essential features are the sand colours, the blue of the sea, the vibrant rainforest greens, the sun yellows, limewashes and brilliant splashes.

Another dominant feature of many of the establishments is the huge number of outdoor table settings. Perfect for this climate, these are the result

Above: The Eduardo's stage.

Right: Aqua Bar window box.

Aqua Bar Goong Yang

Serves 4

20 whole king prawns
4 cups freshly steamed jasmine rice
fresh coriander, cucumber and tomato garnish

Marinade

1 whole clove of garlic peeled and finely chopped
1 tablesp finely chopped fresh coriander root
1½ tablesp white soy sauce   1 pinch cracked black pepper
1 tablesp sugar   1 tablesp cooking oil

Dipping Sauce

1 tablesp chopped fresh garlic
1 tablesp fresh galangal root, finely chopped
1 tablesp fresh lemon grass, finely chopped
1 whole brown onion, finely chopped
2 medium Roma tomatoes, finely diced
1 tablesp Belachan (shrimp paste)
½ cup tomato puree   2 tablesp tamarind juice
2 tablesp sugar   4 tablesp cooking oil
season to taste with fish sauce

Mix marinade ingredients in a bowl and marinate prawns for
2 hours. Barbecue the prawns on a hot grill just before serving.

Heat the cooking oil in a wok until smoking. Fry garlic, galangal,
lemon grass, onion, tomatoes and Belachan until fragrant. Reduce
heat and simmer for 10-15 minutes until sauce thickens. Season
with fish sauce, tamarind juice and sugar.

To assemble, place prawns, rice and garnish on a plate and serve
with dipping sauce on the side.

of a hard fought battle with the council, whose bureaucrats took a long time to come to grips with the realities of our biggest industry, the tourist trade.

At the forefront of Noosa's design and style revolution was Peter Davies, the brooding Welshman, whose mind is always alive with images of Noosa. I have known Peter for many years, and he has always had a Mediterranean eye, which he translates into Noosa style through his most famous medium, sanded render, now exported around the country (and the world) in designer pieces known as Sandbag.

Peter's first design statement in Noosa was at Gaston's (now Cafe Des Amis) in Sunshine Beach where he took North Queensland lawyer cane, soaked and bent it to form furniture, creating an unusual and stunning motif. Unfortunately, its ability to withstand the weather was sorely tested, but by God, it was beautiful.

Leonie's Sand Crab Salad

Serves 6 as starters

6 freshly cooked full sand crabs, all meat removed
1 small Spanish onion, peeled and finely sliced
3 teasp tiny capers
6 tablesp extra virgin olive oil
3 large handfuls of mixed fresh baby salad greens (needs to include rocket for bite)
sea salt and cracked pepper to taste
juice of $\frac{1}{2}$ lime

In a bowl, mix the crab meat, olive oil, capers, onion and salt and pepper to taste. Toss to mix thoroughly and allow to sit for 15-20 minutes.

Toss the salad leaves with lime juice and gently toss in crab mixture. Serve immediately once tossed.

A bowl of roasted peppers cut into strips and marinated olives should accompany this dish.

When my partner Steven Fisher and I started to think about the design of the first Palmer's (now Aqua Bar) there was no one else but Peter who could possibly understand and translate the picture we had in our heads. He transformed a closed up little shop into a streetside trattoria, open and welcoming with its sand ochre walls, blue trims on rendered concrete and details like inset tiny tiles adorning the floor, with the name Palmer's etched in concrete inside the door. Sudden and unexpected touches of the right pink were picked up here and there, windows were trimmed with flower boxes, and there were planter tubs on the street. The place looked fantastic; we prospered and so did Peter, accepting commissions from Going Pasta and later "big" Palmer's, to name but two.

Lyn Brotherton was another important figure in the styling of our restaurants. Lyn is the master of living detail – splashes of raffia, stacks

of lemons, whimsically wrapped napkins, cinnamon stick bundles and backdrops of cardboard and natural textures, always working with available elements. From the early '70s her work began to appear in many of the best restaurants in town. Lyn's signature was her perfect execution of understatement. Lyn was like the Phantom; she worked before opening hours and you would never see her, and often you only noticed her touch when it wasn't there.

Other contributors have been party stylist Kerrie Koch, who could transform your restaurant into Gilligan's Island or Key Largo while you set up the

Above: Detail from Eduardo's.

Right: Aqua Bar.

bar, designer Lynne Tanner, whose stunning hand painted originals spice up the tables and walls of several leading restaurants (and whose handiwork appears on the cover of this book).

The streetside cafes are our most enduring style statement. It all began with Cafe Le Monde, which originally opened as Damiani's in the late '70s. This was stylish enough in itself, but when it later became Le Monde it established the benchmark for alfresco eating. The cafe was the brainchild of Luc Turschwell, who was determined to bring to Noosa some of the avante garde atmosphere of Parisian cafe society. Le Monde has grown and changed over the years, but it retains its original style, with spunky waitresses rushing from table to table with baby computer terminal in hand, and local musicians belting out jazz or blues.

Up the other end of the street (who knows which end is the "Paris" end?) is La Sabbia, which rose Phoenix-like from the ashes of Belmondo's under the direction of the ubiquitous Luc Turschwell. Here he runs a very sleek Euro-cafe with tables all facing the street, as they do in Paris.

LEONIE'S RICH TOMATO SAUCE

A great sauce for pasta, on top of bruschetta or minestrone, with your schnitzel, or anywhere you want the wonderful taste of tomato.

virgin olive oil   1 onion finely chopped
1 carrot finely chopped   1 stick celery finely chopped
8-10 fresh tomatoes skinned & mashed
1 clove garlic crushed
1 tablesp each basil, oregano, parsley chopped.
salt & pepper

Lightly fry vegetables and garlic in oil until soft. Add tomatoes and herbs. Simmer 40 minutes until flavours meld. Season to taste.

To skin tomatoes, score lightly, through skin on base and plunge briefly into boiling water. Strain and peel.

Luc's food style is an important element, but La Sabbia is really all about sitting for hour after hour, watching the passing parade, playing backgammon, sipping on a short black or a white wine. An interesting touch is the streetside creperie, operated by Carlos Ferdinandini, a long-time Peruvian local who never seems to age.

Almost next door, the Aqua Bar has blossomed since we first knocked out the front wall and called it Palmer's. This is Noosa's most in-your-face on-the-street cafe. It's impossible to walk by it; you must walk through it. The indoor and outdoor sections are connected by a table that makes a statement about the Aqua Bar's casual and comfortable style, as well as announcing the influences in the cooking by the presence of a bottle of oil and a bunch of fresh chillies or a pot of Singapore orchids and some lemongrass shoots.

Midway along Hastings Street, on a paved piazza, is Aroma's – not the first of Robyn Horley and Chris Bryant's popular coffee houses but one of the most popular. The comfortable chairs and tables sprawl across the piazza, while inside the carefully-cultivated feeling of age predominates. The smell of roasted coffee is as enticing as the selection of cakes, tarts and cookies lined up like soldiers in a glass-fronted cabinet. At the rear of this island of deco style is a cocktail bar full of amusing features, casually but purposefully thrown together. Here the margaritas and bloody marys are thrown down while the problems of the world are routinely solved.

Sails, in the elbow of Main Beach, looks out over the whole bay. Straight up the grassy slope by the tree under which Stef and I were married, you can enter Sails from the beach, togs dripping, sarong stuck against the body, sandy feet and full of thirst. The room has the sunbleached colours of a Portsea bathing box, and diners can watch the passing parade on the beach or the surfers at First Point. Inside less is more. Proprietor Lyndon Simmons wisely realised that the view was the greatest attraction and kept the room simple and functional.

Out of town in the village of Eumundi, David Baillie has created a stage of his own in the century-old bakery on Memorial Drive. Bartu Jimba, now three years old is heavily Bali-influenced. Although he never trained as a chef, David has travelled widely, always combining his love of food and adventure, which led him to take on cooking jobs, culminating in 10 years working in New York restaurants. Locally, he worked at Misty's of Montville and The Jetty. At Bartu Jimba, David's stage looks out over the village of artists and artisans, and from its garden tables diners can watch the hustle and bustle of the Saturday markets.

There are many more places and people who have helped create Noosa's eating "stage", but these are a representative sample of the places that best express that undefinable quality that is "Noosa".

Above: Scenes from La Sabbia.

Below: Upstairs at Saltwater.

Opposite top: Aqua Bar details.

Opposite below: Outdoor setting at the Spirit House.

LEONIE'S ROASTED PORTERHOUSE TONNATO

With boiled new potatoes and tuna mayonnaise

Serves 6

1kg/2¼lb cleaned porterhouse
4 tablesp extra virgin olive oil
freshly ground black pepper

Pre heat oven to 240°C/475°F

Rub beef all over with the olive oil and sprinkle with pepper. Put in a roasting pan and roast 15 minutes. Remove from oven and rest in its pan.

Boiled New Potatoes

Allow 4-6 per person

Boil in skins in salted water. When cooked place in a bowl and toss with chopped parsley and a little olive oil.

Tuna Mayonnaise

150gm/5oz of canned tuna in oil
3 anchovy fillets canned in oil
3 tablesp capers   1 lemon juiced
400ml/14fl oz good mayonnaise

Place mayonnaise in food processor with broken up tuna, anchovy fillets, capers and lemon juice. Blend together. Add a little cold water to pouring consistency.

Assemble

Slice eye fillet thinly and arrange in a circle around plates. Pile potatoes in the centre, drizzle mayonnaise over the beef and scatter crispy fried capers (following page) over the potatoes.

Fried Capers

3 tablesp capers

Drain capers and dust in plain flour.
Fry quickly in hot olive oil until crunchy, 1-2 minutes.
Remove and drain.

LEONIE'S SPANISH GARLIC MAYONNAISE

Makes 1¼ cups. Serve with Leonie's Bits (page 140).

1 egg yolk at room temperature   1 cup Spanish olive oil
5 garlic cloves   3-4 teasp white wine vinegar
sea salt and freshly ground pepper

Place the egg yolk in the blender with the roughly chopped
garlic, pinch of sea salt and 1 tablesp of oil. Blend vigorously until
the garlic is blended into the oil. With the motor on, very slowly
add the rest of the oil in a thin stream until all the oil is taken up.
Season with salt, pepper and vinegar.

BARTU JIMBA OYSTERS TROPICANA

Entree: serves 4

2 dozen freshly shucked oysters
1 red paw paw   1 lime
chopped chilli and coriander

Paw Paw Salsa

Finely dice the red paw paw and add the juice of ½ the lime.
Mix in chopped chilli and coriander to taste.
Fill each oyster with salsa, serve on crushed ice with lime wedges.

THE PRODUCE

THE SUBTROPICAL CLIMATE of the Sunshine Coast and the rich and fertile soil of the hinterland make it ideal for growing warm climate produce, and as the restaurant market for such exotic products as ginger, chillies, coriander, kaffir limes, tumeric and galangal grew, so too did the number of small, experimental farms tucked away in the hills.

Now, in the late 1990s, the cottage industry has grown to such an extent that local producers are exporting their wares interstate and even overseas. Locally, the availability of this range of produce has inspired greater creativity and given us flexibility in our menus.

Examples of these producers abound, but given the limitations of space, I have selected a few who seem to me to represent the best local food.

Irish-Italian Andy Donnalan bakes bread on his property at Eudlo, near Nambour. He says of himself: "I am a humble baker. I learnt to bake bread when I was 11, watching my mother at the wood-fired oven my father and I built for her."

These days Andy bakes up to 500 loaves a day, not with a recipe as such but using his hands to feel the moisture and the texture of the mix. When he has finished baking he does the deliveries himself (currently servicing at least eight Noosa restaurants) so as to keep in touch with

LEONIE'S AVOCADO VICHYSSOISE

Vichyssoise, although old hat is a delightful chilled soup. With a puree of avocado added and some fresh diced prawns and smoked salmon crowning the dish, it's as good today as it ever was.

Vichyssoise

4 medium sized leeks cut lengthwise and cleaned under running
water to remove all dirt, then diced
2 white onions peeled and diced
90gm/3oz butter
500gm/18oz large potatoes peeled and diced
1ltre/36fl oz water
sea salt and white pepper to taste
250ml/9fl oz pouring cream
fresh chives or parsley

Avocado Puree

3 large ripe but slightly firm avocados, peeled, seeded and roughly chopped. Puree with ½ cup of cold vichyssoise stock.

Prawns or Smoked Salmon

250gm/9oz fresh small prawns, peeled and chopped,
or 250gm/9oz salmon chopped.

Heat butter in stockpot, add leeks and onions and sweat covered for 5 minutes until transparent.

Add potatoes and water and bring to the boil, reduce and simmer, stirring occasionally. When potatoes are soft, cool a little, strain liquid into a bowl and put potato mix through food processor to smooth.

Mix potatoes and liquid together well and then when cold mix in avocado puree and cream.

Season with salt and pepper and whisk to mix well. Set bowl over ice in fridge to chill.

To serve, ladle into pasta bowls (flat ones). Crown portion of prawns or salmon in the centre and sprinkle generously with freshly cut chives or chopped parsley.

Wonderful with warm and crispy bread.

LEONIE'S WA WA SALAD

With Baked Pumpkin and Toasted Walnuts

Take ½kg/18oz Qld Blue Pumpkin, skin and dice (2½cm/
1inch cubes)
Wa Wa salad greens 200grm/7oz (or mixed salad greens)
olive oil
100gm/3½oz parmesan cheese shaved
¼ teasp paprika
¼ teasp cummin
150grm/5oz walnuts
Balsamic vinegar
salt and pepper

In a baking tray, toss pumpkin with enough olive oil to coat, add the paprika and cummin. Bake in preheated oven 200°C/400°F until nicely baked but still firm to the bite. At the same time, very lightly oil the walnuts and roast until crunchy – don't burn. Cool pumpkin and walnuts, toss with salad greens, shaved parmesan and season to taste. Dress with a little olive oil and Balsamic vinegar.

the needs of his clients. He is particularly proud of the quality of his crust. Oh, and Andy believes that all business negotiations should be done over a glass of Guinness and a few strong short blacks.

The Buderim Ginger Co-operative was born in a blacksmith's shop in Buderim in 1941, as the result of the war interrupting ginger imports from China. Local farmers had been growing ginger for some time, but the suddenly increased demand meant they had to get serious. Half a century later it is a publicly-listed company supplying 18 countries.

Above: Wa Wa salad.   *Right: Baker Andy Donnellan.*

Opposite: Local herba and spices; Cardiman pods, ground spices, chillies.

In the early days the main product lines were the sweet variety, such as crystallised ginger. But as times and tastes changed, the company moved more into savoury products like pickled ginger and fresh crushed ginger and lemon. Today, the modern plant at Yandina processes ginger supplied to quota by farms within a 60-kilometre radius, and the Buderim Ginger tourist facility explains ginger production to countless visitors, helping to spread the word about ginger.

In Noosa's restaurants, Buderim Ginger products are used side by side with fresh ginger to create a range of tastes from modern Asian to old-fashioned ice cream sundaes.

PINEAPPLE BRULEE CHEESECAKE

Pastry base

200gm/7oz plain flour
60gm/2oz icing sugar
pinch of salt
175gm/6oz soft unsalted butter
2 egg yolks

Mix dry ingredients. Add butter and egg yolks one at a time, do not over work. Leave for 30 minutes.

Place pastry in fluted 30cm/12inch tart ring and line using palm of hand.

Pre-bake for 15 minutes at 150°C/300°F.

Filling

2 eggs whole
2 egg yolks
$^1/_2$ teasp vanilla essence
500gm/18oz cream cheese
$^3/_4$ cup brown sugar
1 tablesp lemon juice
1 tablesp pineapple juice

Place eggs and sugar in Kitchen Whizz and mix until pale, follow with cream cheese and juices.

Pour mix into pre-baked tart shell and bake for 1 hour at 160°C/310°F. Leave to cool overnight.

Before serving dust with brown sugar and place under hot grill to caramelise.

LEONIE'S COMPOTE OF GUAVA

1kg/2$^{1}/_{4}$lb firm but ripe guavas
Juice of 1-2 limes, strained
1 cinnamon stick
2 cardamom pods, crushed
500ml/27fl oz sugar syrup

Note: for sugar syrup
1kg/2$^{1}/_{4}$lb castor sugar
1ltre/54fl oz water

Bring to boil together in a saucepan for 10minutes. Can be sealed in a jar and kept for 3 days in the fridge.

Wash and dry the guavas. Peel halve and core them and place peel and seed centres in pan with 150ml/5fl oz (approx) water, bring to boil and simmer 5-10 minutes until very soft. Strain through fine sieve and add to the sugar syrup with lime juice.

Place guava halves in the syrup and gently bring to the boil, (must be done gently or the fruit will disintegrate) with the cinnamon stick and cardamom pods. Leave in pan to cool.

Bottle in preserving jars and use with plain yoghurt for breakfast or as an accompaniment to coconut cake.

If you can find guava in the market or on someone's tree do try this recipe. The guava has the most wonderful pervasive smell that will fill your kitchen and it really is delicious eating. The strawberry guava is I think the pick of the crop. This recipe is also stunning with half guava and half peach (cut in quarters, peeled and stoned).

Since 1990 Lucy Connop and Jack Hogan have grown specialty vegetables, principally for the restaurant market from their farm near Cooroy. In fact, their company, Mary Valley Plantation, was born one evening in the 1980s when they dined at Little Palmer's and considered the possibility that there might be a local market for interesting vegetables.

From humble beginnings, using Lucy's specialised knowledge from the Burnley College of Horticulture in Melbourne, they slowly built their business, and now produce minimally-processed specialty vegetables, many of Asian origin, sold in modified atmosphere bags. They now supply a good part of southern Queensland and are about to establish a co-operative to provide better lines of supply to restaurants. They have trademarked their

LEONIE'S ROASTED BABY CHICKENS WITH BREAD STUFFING

Serves 4

2 whole baby chickens size 9
4 slices country style bread cubed (1¼cm/½inch)
200 gm/7oz smoked bacon cut thick and diced
2 cloves garlic peeled and finely chopped
approx. 6 sprigs each Italian parsley, lemon thyme, rosemary and
oregano. Rough chop about half of each
olive oil
½ onion peeled and diced
50gm/2oz softened butter
dash white wine vinegar
salt and pepper to taste

Wash and pat dry baby chickens. Make sure all innards are removed.

Take a wide frying pan, well heated, add a little olive oil, when hot toss in garlic and bread and toss about until bread is lightly tanned. Add onion, bacon and fry 1-2 minutes. Add chopped herbs and white wine vinegar. Take off heat and season with salt and pepper. Mix together.

Stuff the birds full but not too tight.

Heat oven to 200°C/400°F. Have ready a roasting dish (I use a terracotta), big enough to hold the birds. Place the sprigs of herbs on the bottom and place the chickens on top.

Rub chickens with a little salt, black pepper, olive oil and a little of the butter. Roast in middle of the oven for 15 minutes. Baste again with a little more butter and roast another 15 minutes. Baste with last of butter and roast another 15 minutes.

Pour off juices and rest chickens for 10 minutes.

Put the roasting juices in a small frying pan and deglaze with a little wine vinegar.

Cut the birds in half along the backbone. Plate and pour over a little of the juice. Serve with a fresh tomato salad drizzled with olive oil, balsamic vinegar and sea salt, and wok seared silverbeet. Precede with starter of salad of celery hearts.

LEONIE'S WOK-SEARED SILVERBEET

(Actually Leonie and Phil Mitchell's recipe.)

Wash one bunch of silverbeet in chilled salted water, maybe changing the water a couple of times (or use English spinach leaves uncut).

Remove stem and cut into 6cm long rectangles. Place in a lettuce spinner and spin a couple of times.

Place a wok on high heat and drizzle in a little sesame oil. When the oil just begins to smoke, throw the silverbeet in with some care. Toss for a couple of minutes. Season.

Serve immediately.

SALAD OF CELERY HEARTS AND GOATS' CHEESE

Take young celery hearts, cut in half length-wise, and serve with a fresh mild goats' cheese.

Top with a dressing on lemon juice, mixed with a dash of Dijon mustard and some extra virgin olive oil.

Wa Wa Mixes, a seasonal salad mix and a mix of Asian greens for stir-fries, and I can tell you I have never seen a southern tourist see Wa Wa on the menu and not order it!

Meanwhile, across the cane-fields at Yandina, Peter and Helen Brierty's Avant Gardens hydroponic farm features endless rows of "window boxes" overflowing with lush green lettuce and herbs of many varieties, supplying their own Spirit House restaurant, other restaurants and supermarkets.

Garnisha Curries at Boreen Point is the realisation of a lifelong dream for Tim and Claire Warren. The

Above: Leonie's baby chook.

LEONIE'S SASHIMI RECIPE

Serves 2

200gm/7oz freshest possible tuna, sliced wafer thin
150ml/5fl oz mayonnaise
wasabi powder mixed to paste with water (to taste)
30ml/1fl oz Tamari soy sauce
juice $\frac{1}{2}$ lemon
Buderim pickled gingers – pale pieces and bright straws

Mix the mayonnaise with wasabi paste, soy sauce, lemon juice.
Whisk to mix and if necessary add a little water to pouring
consistency. Put into a squeeze bottle.

Lay tuna slices to overlap and cover plates. Squeeze mayonnaise
from bottle over tuna in a diamond pattern and lay ginger in
between in alternating colours. Serve and eat immediately.

LEONIE'S ANGEL HAIR PASTA AND ZUCCHINI

Serves 4 as starters

250gm/9oz Saffron Angel Hair Pasta or very fine spaghetti
2 medium zucchinis grated with skin on
1 medium leek, washed of dirt and sliced finely
2 cloves garlic, peeled and finely chopped
2 fresh chillies, seeded and finely chopped (optional)
$\frac{1}{3}$ cup virgin olive oil
salt and freshly ground pepper to taste
grated fresh parmesan or crumbled gorgonzola

Bring a generous size pot of water to a good boil, add the pasta
and cook al dente, drain. In a heavy based hot frying pan put a
little olive oil, saute garlic and leek until just transparent. Add
zucchini and toss a couple of times to briefly cook 1-2 minutes.
In a bowl put the rest of the olive oil and the fresh chilli. Toss in
the pasta and zucchini, toss well to mix. Season with salt and
pepper. Pass the parmesan or gorgonzola separately.

GRILLED CALF'S LIVER

4 fresh trimmed, cleaned thin slices of liver, flour dusted
2 thinly sliced onions
6 tablesp olive oil   2 tablesp unsalted butter
1 tablesp sage leaves   red wine vinegar

Heat $\frac{2}{3}$ oil in frying pan, add onions and cook over medium
heat until limp and browned (stir frequently). Remove onions.
Increase heat to high, add rest of oil to pan, when sizzling add
liver. Cook 1 minute each side, add onions, season and cook
1 minute longer. Transfer liver and onions to a platter, add a dash
of vinegar to pan, add butter, stir together, take off heat, add sage
leaves and spoon over liver. Serve immediately.

herbs and spice farm grew from his love of chutneys and pickles and anything spicy. Tim's mother-in-law, who grew up in Poona, passed on some old family curry recipes and Tim and Claire started experimenting with spice products to sell at the Eumundi Markets. Four years on, they are now supplying many outlets along the east coast.

I personally think that Garnisha pastes are exquisitely aromatic and work wonderfully in Indian dishes. Why would you go to the trouble of making your own spice mixes when experts like Tim and Claire have already done it?

It would make a great story to say here that only local seafood is used in Noosa's restaurants, but it would also be a lie. The vagaries of supply and the huge demand, the bureaucrats of the Queensland Fish Management Authority, and the fact that we live on a shallow river in which access to outside fishing grounds is dependent on weather, all dictate that seafood from other regions is also served. However, Rod Fitzgerald's Arctic Ice at Noosaville offers a high proportion of local Queensland fish and shellfish, supplemented by clams and mussels from Victoria and Tasmania, calamari from New Zealand and Tasmanian Atlantic salmon.

Over the past seven years the company has found a positive gourmet seafood direction, and Rod takes pride in handling quality local fish, like Mooloolaba tuna, Noosa River mullet, whiting and garfish.

Finally, Noosa has more ice cream parlours than any other place on earth. Arguably, it also has the best. Massimo's, tucked into the front of Netanya Noosa Resort, serves ice cream which reminds me of the gelati shops of Florence. Quite rightly so, too, because Massimo is an Italian. He makes his own ice cream and gelati from pure ingredients in natural fruit flavours, like watermelon and passionfruit, and the more traditional Italian flavours like chocolate, baci and malaga, which is a fabulous blend of raisins and marsala.

THE TWISTS

IT'S PROBABLY GOING a bit far to say that Noosa is a twisted society, but we do seem to have taken some unusual detours over the years, in food and drink as much as other aspects of our lifestyles.

The restrictive rules of city life just do not apply, and this has been evident since the very early days, when cafes sprang up overnight with no thought given to council permissions or any other bureaucratic intervention. Noosa back then was a good times place, and nothing much has changed, though our establishments may have grown a little more sophisticated (and legitimate).

The free and easy lifestyle inspires experimentation – bold colours on restaurant walls, crazy motifs, alfresco cafes that block the footpath, food that defies traditional categorisation, cocktails you wouldn't dare to drink in Sydney or Melbourne. This is a holiday town where we work at making it party time all the time.

Come with me now and let's check out some of Noosa's twists.

The Noosaville Riviera is taking shape down on the river-front where residents and shopkeepers wake every morning to the sounds of the developers' hammers. (Oh please don't spoil it!) This is where it all began with Maisie Monsour's Favourite Cafe, and it is the eat street of the

Leonie's Bits

Poisson Cru

500gm/18oz bite size fresh fish pieces
fresh lime juice
1 onion chopped finely
salt

Cover the fish pieces completely with lime juice, onion and salt and refrigerate 2-3 hours. Drain off juice and use to make a dressing with:

150gm/5oz coconut milk
2 tomatoes seeded and diced
1 red chilli seeded and chopped
1 small bunch of chives finely chopped
1-2 heads of witlof, washed and trimmed

Pour over fish and refrigerate again for a couple of hours.
Serve at room temperature, a little mound in each witlof leaf.

Sesame Coated Zucchini Batons

4 medium zucchini cut into batons 4cm/1½inch long. Dip in flour, then egg and milk wash, then sesame seeds. Deep fry in hot oil until golden brown, lift out gently with slotted spoon. Drain, serve hot with garlic mayonnaise (page 121).

Stuffed Green Olives

Stone Queen green olives, stuff with a mix of mashed soft cheese and finely chopped toasted almonds. Dip in flour, then egg and milk wash, then fine breadcrumbs. Deep fry in hot oil until just golden. Drain and serve with glasses of chilled sherry.

LEONIE'S GNOCCHI

Parisian Gnocchi

This is a light and delicate gnocchi, really like a souffle. They must be served immediately straight from the baking dish at the table. Serve as an entree or luncheon dish with a crisp salad of greens.

1 cup milk   6 tablesp unsalted butter
1 cup plain flour   4 eggs
$\frac{1}{2}$ cup freshly grated parmesan
$\frac{1}{4}$ teasp cayenne pepper
2 cups of a rich smooth bechamel sauce, keep warm

Preheat oven to 220°C/425°F

Put milk, butter and pinch salt into a large saucepan and bring to boil. When butter has melted add the flour all at once and stir the mixture vigorously over low heat with wooden spoon until the dough forms a ball and leaves the sides of the pan.
Stir 1-2 minutes over low heat and remove from heat.

Cool 5 minutes.

Place mixture in food processor and process 15 seconds. Add the eggs all at once and process 30-40 seconds until dough is smooth and shiny. Add $\frac{3}{4}$ of the cheese and pulse a few times to combine. Do not overprocess the dough.

Cover the bottom of 30cm/12inch gratin dish or casserole with half the bechamel. With fingers dipped in cold water, form the dough into golf ball sized gnocchi and put in gratin dish, with a little space between each. Sprinkle the gnocchi with remaining cheese and cover with the remaining bechamel.

Bake gnocchi 25-30 minutes or until well risen and top is just crusting brown. Do not open oven for first 25 minutes or gnocchi will fall. Serve immediately.

future, with cafes, delis, wok shops and restaurants springing up the length of Gympie Terrace and adjacent streets.

Anita's was an early starter just around the corner, and former Hastings Street restaurateur Grenville Duckworth has moved his Grenny's Seawater Cafe into a shop-front opposite the river. This little BYO and takeaway has a few tables spilling out onto the street, and a house specialty befitting the seafarers' setting. Grenny's seafood Marseilles is a peasant dish of prawns, bug tails, mussels and crab simmered in garlic, white wine and fish stock. Delicious.

Also along the river-front you'll find Lemon Grass Cafe, the Noosa River Deli and So Wok. This last is one of two new wave wok shops in Noosa, and both are storming the take-away market with their hot and spicy, cheap and cheerful laksas and soups.

Speaking of twisted, former boat-builder and town scalliwag Geoff Hall and wife Charmaine started a joinery business specialising (appropriately) in bars and restaurant fittings. Geoff built the beautiful curved bar at Palmer's.

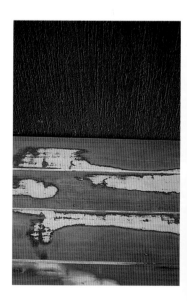

Above left: Grenny.

Above right: So Wok.

Left: Hastings Street fruit barrow.

These days Geoff and Char have transferred their energies to another twist in the food racket, opening the stylish Cooking Company in Noosa Junction. This shop specialises in practical designer cook wear for both professional and home kitchens. In his spare time, Geoff still plies the river in his restored kauri pine boat The Neptune, which is always well-provisioned with rum, beautifully presented food and good wine. Yummy!

Top: Palmer's cocktails.

Above: Anyone for a Pimms?

PALMER'S PINK GRAPEFRUIT MARGARITA

15ml/$\frac{1}{2}$oz gold Tequila
15ml/$\frac{1}{2}$oz Campari
15ml/$\frac{1}{2}$oz Cointreau
juice of 1 medium grapefruit
2 teasp salt
1 cocktail shaker
1 champagne flute
cracked ice

Dip rim of champagne flute in grapefruit juice, allow excess to run off, crust in salt and leave to set.

Pour Tequila, Campari, Cointreau and grapefruit juice into the shaker with the cracked ice.

Shake well, strain into salt-rimmed flute and serve.

AROMA'S ESPRESSO NUT SUNDAE

In a blender add a small scoop of ice

Add chilled short black (or 30ml/1oz of very strong plunger coffee)

15ml/$\frac{1}{2}$oz Frangelico
15ml/$\frac{1}{2}$oz Butterscotch Schnapps
30ml/1oz Kahlua
60ml/2oz cream.

Blend 30 secs

Pour into cocktail glass – sprinkle with roasted coffee beans.

Stef's Cocktails

Pimms for Six

Fill a 2ltre/74fl oz glass jug with ice cubes. Pour in ⅓ bottle of Pimms No 1 Cup.

Add finely cut slices of lime, lemon, orange and cucumber. Then fill jug with ½ dry ginger ale, ½ lemonade. Finish with sprigs of fresh mint. Stir and let steep before serving.

Mango Daiquiri

Put in a blender 2 handfulls of crushed ice, 1 large Bowen mango peeled and stoned. Add 60ml/2oz Bacardi rum and 30ml/1oz Cointreau. Pour into a stemmed flute and garnish simply with a sprig of fresh mint.

Tom's Cocktails

Tom Sykes turned out to be one of Stef's best protegés in the field of cocktail "mixology" (style, service, speed).

Campari Crusta

Sugar crust the rim of a champagne flute. In a shaker of cracked ice, mix 30ml/1oz Campari, 15ml/½oz Cointreau and 60ml/2oz orange juice. Shake vigorously and pour with gusto.

Citrus Twist

In a blender with a handful of crushed ice, add 30ml/1oz Stollichnaya vodka, 15ml/½oz Cointreau, the juices of ½ Tahitian lime and 2 lemons. Blend until frozen crush consistency and serve in a chilled flute. Garnish with a twist of fresh lime.

THE MEMORIES

*50 years of tears, beers
and rollicking good times
in Australia's favourite
resort village*

Barry's

Rio's crew

Vale Danny

DOOK'S GARDEN
WINE—BAR BISTRO

OPENING PRESS NIGHT
SATURDAY 15TH DECEMBER FROM SUNSET

Your Hosts — Greg McDermott & Dick Thorne

SUNSHINE BEACH ROAD, NOOSA JUNCTION

Hey Bill

Belmondo's Mark I

Molly goes to Rio's

Hastings Street

Hot Gillie's

Palmer's party night

Hollywood Bob

Woody, Pete and Pete

RECIPE INDEX